Musical Openings

Using music in the language classroom

Pilgrims

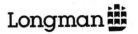

Longman

David Cranmer and Clement Laroy

Addison Wesley Longman Limited
Edinburgh Gate, Harlow
Essex CM20 2JE, England
and Associated Companies throughout the world.

© Longman Group UK Limited 1992

This book is produced in association with Pilgrims
Language Courses Limited of Canterbury, England.

First published 1992
Fourth impression 1998

Set in 10/12 ITC Cheltenham Book

Produced through Longman Malaysia,

British Library Cataloguing in Publication Data
Cranmer, David
    Musical Openings: Using Music in the
    Language Classroom
    I. Title II. Laroy, Clement
    407.1

ISBN 0 582 07504 1

Acknowledgements
We are indebted to Cambridge University Press for
permission to reproduce an adapted extract from
International Business English by L Jones and
R Alexander (1989).

We are grateful to the following for permission to
reproduce copyright material:

The National Gallery for page 76 (above);
National Portrait Gallery for page 69 (below);
The Tate Gallery, London for page 77 (below);
Courtesy of the Board of Trustees of the V&A for
pages 76 (below) and 77 (above); Joseph Laroy for
page 62.

The drawing on pages 49, 50, 52, 53 and 55 are based
on a set conceived by Paulo Figueiredo, a student.
Redrawn by Chris Pavely.

Illustrations
Cover illustrated by Grahame Baker

A letter from the Series Editors

Dear Teacher,

This series of teachers' resource books has developed from Pilgrims' involvement in running courses for learners of English and for teachers and teacher trainers.

Our aim is to pass on ideas, techniques and practical activities which we know work in the classroom. Our authors, both Pilgrims teachers and like-minded colleagues in other organisations, present accounts of innovative procedures which will broaden the range of options available to teachers working within communicative and humanistic approaches.

We would be very interested to receive your impressions of the series. If you notice any omissions that we ought to rectify in future editions, or if you think of any interesting variations, please let us know. We will be glad to acknowledge all contributions that we are able to use.

Seth Lindstromberg
Series Editor

Mario Rinvolucri
Series Consultant

Pilgrims Language Courses
Canterbury
Kent
CT1 3HG
England

David Cranmer

David was always going to be a musician. He began to learn the piano at the age of six and the organ at sixteen. He read Music at Sidney Sussex College, Cambridge and went on to study Musicology at King's College, London. He then began a career in English Language Teaching, working in Britain, Iran, Holland and, since 1981, as a teacher and teacher-trainer at the British Council, Lisbon. He has published many articles on ELT, including two in *Practical English Teaching* and contributions to *At the Chalkface* (Edward Arnold 1985) and *More Recipes for Tired Teachers* (Addison-Wesley 1991). He is also editor of the *British Council Newsletter for Portuguese Teachers of English*. In recent years he has resumed his professional activities as an organist and musicologist, and is currently working on his doctoral thesis *Opera in Portugal 1793–1828.*

Clement Laroy

Clem attended his first concert at the Brussels World Fair in 1958, when he was fifteen. He started teaching at the age of 19. When he was twenty he left Belgium for five years to teach in Africa, where he started using songs and the treble recorder in his English lessons. Back in Belgium, while studying at university (Germanic philology), he was involved in the production of educational television programmes on scientific and technical English. Later, he worked in the Department of Applied Linguistics of the University of Brussels (Institut de Phonétique) before becoming a teacher trainer. He met his future wife in Saigon in 1973. They have two children who could not live without music.

David and Clem met during a Pilgrims course for teacher trainers organised by the British Council in Canterbury in 1985.

Dedication

To all our friends, students and colleagues who have helped us to understand music and ourselves better through what we have written here.

Contents

Index of activities

Epigraph

'What do you want to do with your violin?'
'Make it speak! That's the only thing I can do with it.'
Isaac Stern (BBC Music Review, November 1990)

Introduction

WHAT IS THIS BOOK ABOUT?

The idea of using music in the teaching of languages is not a new one. As long as people have learnt languages, songs have played an important role in the learning process, not only in the classroom but in the world outside. Music is such a fundamental manifestation of culture and of the human need to communicate that it is inextricably associated with language.

As the teaching of languages has developed over the years into an increasingly sophisticated art, the use of songs to teach structures, to provide some kind of broader cultural input or for sheer enjoyment has been a constant feature. More recently, we have seen music creeping into class in other ways and for other reasons. In particular, the use of music in the method known as Suggestopedia has awakened teachers to the importance of music as an element of the relaxed classroom. Many teachers who do not necessarily agree with everything in this method nevertheless recognise the value of soothing background music as a means of relaxing a tense class. Listening to music after a hard day's work or a sleepless night brings us to a more receptive state of mind for the language lesson ahead. This book takes the use of songs and lyrics for granted, as a good deal has been written on the subject already. What we have done is to look at music more in terms of its affective nature and its powers of suggestion. Although we have included areas that relate to the Suggestopedic use of music (above all in Activity 1.9 *Background music*), we have concentrated much more on another area that language teachers so far have rarely explored, namely the power of music to stimulate images for the inner eye.

Many people see images in music even unprompted. More importantly for us as language teachers, music acts as a key to the imagination, even with many people who claim to have no imagination at all.

During the nineteenth century there developed a particular kind of music which recognised this power of music to suggest images and was given the name 'programme music'. Although earlier composers (e.g. the sixteenth-century composer Jannequin, who wrote songs that imitated the sounds of birdsong and battle) had touched on the idea, it is essentially the Romantic composers who began to look at this power inherent in music in any systematic kind of way. Preliminary moves in this direction are apparent in pieces such as Beethoven's 'Pastoral' Symphony and Rossini's Overture to *William Tell*, but it is above all Berlioz who developed the art of portraying scenes, people and events in music. Many composers thereafter, most notably perhaps Liszt and Richard Strauss, were attracted to this idea, but the fact is that from a musical point of view programme music was always less than fully successful. No matter what composers did they could not guarantee that the image they were trying to convey would be the image that listeners would form in their own minds.

What to music was an insuperable problem, to us as language teachers is an enormous boon. The ambiguity inherent in what (if anything) music actually conveys provides an instant talking point as soon as there are two or more listeners. For no two people will hear a piece of music in quite the same way, not only because they are different people but because their moods and even physical states may be different. The same person on different occasions may hear the same music in an entirely different way. Our chief objective in this book has been to exploit these differences in listener perception and employ them for language learning purposes. The fact that different people perceive the same piece of music in different ways is crucially important to this book, but equally so is the need people have to tell others and find out from others what they have heard – what we might call a 'curiosity gap' has been created. Now this curiosity gap goes a great deal further than the 'information gap' or 'opinion gap' that much so-called 'communicative' teaching aims to produce, for all too often in these 'communicative' lessons there is absolutely no reason to exchange information or opinions other than that the teacher says so. Our experience with many of the activities we do with music, on the other hand, is that discussion arises spontaneously as an automatic response to the music the students have been listening to and the task they have been doing.

Central to our main technique is the concept of visualisation with the inner eye: the ability to form images in the mind in response to a musical stimulus. It is what could be called the 'Fantasia' principle, that is to say the principle by which Walt Disney was able to create the famous film *Fantasia*. In that film he took music and put cartoon images to it as a realisation of the visual fantasies that came to his mind as he heard the music. Thus Mickey Mouse, for example, acted out the role of the Apprentice in Dukas's *The Sorcerer's Apprentice* as Disney imagined it. A similar principle applies in ballet (and for this reason some ballet music is excellent for language work), where the composer tries to convey some kind of story or scene in music which the choreographer has to realise visually in the form of dance. The same principle in reverse applies when pre-existing music is used as the soundtrack for a film – in some cases the music is so well chosen (e.g. some of Kubrick's films) that the music becomes almost inseparable from the film thereafter. This happened, for example, with his film *2001 A Space Odyssey* and the opening of Richard Strauss's *Also sprach Zarathustra*.

TWO RESERVATIONS YOU MAY HAVE

As you may have gathered, the kind of music we are talking about is, by and large, European-based classical music. It is important to realise, however, that it need not be necessarily so, nor need it be restricted to music with an obvious programme. Any music that is evocative of images or associations will do just as well. We have chosen some music from other cultures precisely to make this point. Western classical music is, nevertheless, particularly suitable, not least because of its being generally available and appreciated throughout the world, in a way that, say, Nigerian, Vietnamese, or even Indian music is not, except to people in those parts of the world or to specialists. But what about pop and rock music? After all, that is what most of our students listen to and like; they generally *don't* like classical music. What we have found, though, is that for the purpose of stimulating images in the inner eye, pop and rock music tend not to work well. Words are distracting (we rarely use vocal classical music for this same reason) and the range of images stimulated is much more limited. On the other hand, when we have used classical music we have not been greeted with the adverse teenage reaction that you might expect. The reasons for this are actually quite clear. We are not asking our students to like or make profound comments about the music (unlike in the music lesson), but simply to respond to it, and a negative response is every bit as valid for language learning purposes as a positive one. To take an example of what actually happened in one lesson – we asked the class to listen to a piece of music and say what colour it was for them. One student said, 'Black, because I don't like classical music.' In terms of language learning, this was just as useful a response as 'Green, because it reminds me of trees and forests' or 'Orange, because I hear the setting sun'. Yet the plain fact is that this student was very much an exception, and a very important spin-off of our work has been to bring many, many people (especially teenagers) to classical music who would formerly have rejected it out of hand.

Another reservation some teachers have is that some people just don't like music or are quite unable to visualise from a musical stimulus. This is sometimes a problem, though not a common one, in our experience. We would like to make the point, however, that the same is to some extent true of any classroom activity. Some people don't like doing grammar exercises, role plays or whatever, and some people are quite unable to write essays or act in drama activities. Yet it does not stop teachers doing all of these things with students, not with every class all of the time, but selectively. What has been much more important to us, though, is the number of students who in the past have been too shy or apathetic to contribute much to class, but who through music have suddenly come to life. Many of our colleagues have commented on this aspect of our work.

WHAT IS IN THIS BOOK?

This book is divided into eight chapters, each consisting of a series of activities. Within each activity we have followed a standard format.

In the margin you will find the level, focus and average duration, plus an indication of any extras you need beyond a cassette recorder and cassette(s).

In many instances we have written a paragraph at the head of the activity to give you further information about the rationale behind the activity, side benefits and, in a very few instances, warnings of possible dangers. In this opening paragraph we have also mentioned the music you need if the activity requires one or more specific pieces, or if we have exemplified the technique with a particular piece in mind. Otherwise there is a Suggested Music heading at the end of the activity.

If you need to prepare anything in advance, we have indicated this under the heading Preparation. The Procedure follows and is broken down into steps. After this in some cases you will find Extensions – additional tasks to take the activity further – and/or Variations – other similar techniques for what is essentially the same activity. Sometimes there are also Notes – further information we feel you should have.

Whenever we have used a particular source to help us write an activity and whenever we have learnt an activity from someone else, we have indicated this under an Acknowledgements heading.

In a number of activities we have included samples of student work, giving the student's name and, where possible, age. We have left these uncorrected to give you an idea of the kind of language they really produce. As you will see, the content is often so rich that the errors seem very trivial in comparison.

WHAT IS ON THE ACCOMPANYING CASSETTE?

We have gone to some lengths to include as wide a range of music as possible for our activities, in particular to include music of as many nationalities as possible. It would take you many weeks to hear all the music we have mentioned. Our task in selecting music for the cassette has therefore been difficult. We have followed two main principles.

Firstly, we have chosen a lot of short pieces and excerpts rather than a few longer ones, so that you have *some* music on the cassette for many of the activities. Secondly, we have tried to include pieces we regard as essential for you to use the book, but which are not readily available. In the remaining cases, either the music suggested is well known and easy to obtain (in shops, borrowed from colleagues, students and friends) or we have given several suggestions, one or other of which you should be able to find without great difficulty.

Music included on the cassette is indicated in the book by a cassette symbol (▭).

SOME IMPORTANT GENERAL PRINCIPLES

1 The place of music in your teaching programme

Although some of the activities in this book work well as 'one-off' lessons, that is not what we really intend. In all cases you should regard them as activities that help you to teach whatever you want to teach anyway. They should complement other activities you use as a matter of course in your teaching.

You will not necessarily like all of our activities or the music we have chosen. They are in this book because they work for us and for colleagues who have tried them. Use those that you feel will work for you – very likely over a period of time you will feel more adventurous. We hope too that you will try your own activities with your own kind of music. Maybe you will make a piece of music work that we were unsuccessful with and had to abandon. There is no right or wrong music or activity, only those that work and those that don't. What matters is that you believe in what you are doing. If you do, whatever you try will go well. If you don't, your students will quickly pick up your doubts and things will go wrong. Try activities on yourself first and only use them if they work for you.

2 Equipment

You do not need hi-fi equipment but you will get better results if you have a reasonably good cassette recorder. The small portable recorders used in some classrooms are not good enough unless they reproduce the bass properly as well as the treble. Larger portables (often with twin speakers) such as many teachers and students have for their own use at home are usually perfectly adequate. It is worth bringing your own in or asking your students if one of them would mind bringing theirs in on an occasion when you specially want to use music.

3 Obtaining 'Extras'

We have sometimes suggested photographs and reproductions of paintings among the extra things you need. We have given the source and provided any information you need on where to obtain them.

4 Managing your class

It is probably true of any teaching, but we find it particularly important in our 'music lessons' to be gentle and encouraging, yet firm at times. In most activities there are occasions when we tell you to 'elicit' or 'discuss with your students' or 'ask your students for feedback'. These are all occasions when you are up front and working with the whole class. Encourage *all* your students to participate and answer. Don't let your more extroverted students dominate, and be especially watchful for the shy student who has something to say. This is vital with music-based activities as it is the more sensitive students that feel the music more deeply.

When you monitor your students to see how they are getting on, it is important not to 'hover'. Students, especially when they listen to music, need psychic space and often also need some moments of silence after listening, especially if they are writing in response to the music. It is usually best to be 'availably out of the way', that is, available for their needs (encourage them to call you when they need you) but without invading their thoughts and feelings.

When your students give you feedback in response to music they have just heard, it is very important to regard all responses as equally valid. The way people hear music is highly individual and personal. To invalidate the way someone has heard a piece is tantamount to invalidating the person. Even if the composer made a clear statement of what he was trying to convey, this is not as valid to the listener as their own response. Precisely because of this individuality of response, you will find that each student handles the task at his or her own level, whether linguistic, intellectual or affective. For this reason you will find many of our activities ideal for classes where there is a wide ability range. At the same time, don't be surprised if music brings out unexpected talent from where you least expect it.

The question of error and correction poses something of a dilemma. Responses to music tend to be spontaneous – unstructured and often in the mother tongue. To turn these responses into clear, coherent, grammatically correct English is to risk losing their immediacy. In our activities we have tried to strike a balance. Some activities, especially in Chapters 2 (Talking about music) and 3 (Grammar) demand greater accuracy, while others, mainly in later chapters, lay greater emphasis on the freedom to respond in a less structured way. Others again, such as Activity 4.2 *What else happened?*, start from spontaneous responses and lead on to more controlled work. What is important in all cases is to channel the spontaneous responses, whatever they may be, into the language learning task at hand, whether it is a highly controlled one or a much freer one.

5 Teaching blind or deaf students

Music is an important medium for both the blind and, perhaps surprisingly, the deaf. You probably know that Beethoven went deaf in mid-career and there have been many great musicians who were blind for all or much of their lives. Students who are blind from birth cannot visualise easily, but there are many activities in this book that do not require visualisation. Many students who are considered 'educationally deaf', that is to say suffer serious learning difficulties on account of their deafness, nevertheless have sufficient residual hearing to listen to and enjoy music. Indeed they are often more than usually sensitive to music. So while being aware of the difficulties your blind or deaf students may have, by no means rule out using music in their classes.

CONCLUSION

We never cease to be amazed by the reaction we get from our students as they listen to the music we play. And not only our students but family and friends, other teachers, anybody that has ears to hear. We believe this has to do with the way our activities demand active listening to the music and force the listener to relate to it. There is such a huge difference between listening to, say, Elgar's *Enigma Variations* in the concert hall just for enjoyment, and likely as not distracted by the sweet-paper-rattler in the row behind and the cougher three rows in front, and listening to three of the *Variations* in Activity 5.7 *Friends*, with the task of describing the people we hear in the music. With the guidance of the activity we hear the music in a different and much more profound way, whether we are untrained musically or a musician by profession.

In preparing this book both of us have learnt an enormous amount about music and its effect on people. It has also been an enormous joy to bring so much music to others, many of whom would have remained blocked to music, especially classical music, maybe for the rest of their lives.

Acknowledgements

I would like to thank David Oistrakh, the pygmies of the Ituri forest and the parishioners of a bush church in Shaba (Zaire) for having opened me to music. Thanks also to Almuth Hiemsch, the children and the participants at the International Workcamps in Germany who introduced me to the music of their countries, in particular Germany and Scandinavia. I would also like to express my gratitude to Jean Auquier, librarian at the College of Education and Teacher Training in Morlanwelz, for his help and encouragement. A special word of thanks to my wife and children for helping me to realise what untapped potential there is in music and for their support and patience – Clem.

I would like to thank the friends who encouraged me when the first ideas of using classical music in language teaching were hatching, in particular Tiago Sousa, Miguel Costa e Moura, Maria Natália Coelho, Sheila Ward, John Haycraft, Mike Beaumont and Mario Rinvolucri. This book is the result. Many thanks also to colleagues at the British Council, Lisbon for their valuable suggestions during piloting and to Paulo Simões for his help in printing out the final manuscript – David.

We would both like to thank our students in Belgium, Portugal and Zaire for participating and reacting, and everyone else without whom this book would have been impossible: Bernard Dufeu, The British Council, and the staff of Pilgrims, especially Seth Lindstromberg for his valuable advice and suggestions.

CHAPTER 1

Getting ready

The activities in this chapter will help you to get your students into a positive state of mind for other activities, whether musical or not. Activities 1.1 *Focusing* and 1.2 *Follow the Spiral* are concentration tasks. In later activities in the book we have often advised you to do one of these as a preliminary to or as a part of another activity and we would encourage you to make them a regular part of your lesson.

All of the remaining activities are aimed at modifying the energy level of everyone in the class, yourself included. Activity 1.9 *Background music* aims to create a relaxed atmosphere in class, while the other activities aim to raise the energy level of the class. Use whichever you find appropriate, according to whether your class is over-excited or lethargic. Often students need first to get the energy out of their system (use Activities 1.3–1.8) and then something to calm them down (use Activity 1.9). It is a good idea always to carry with you a cassette with energizing music on one side and relaxing music on the other, ready to use whenever the need arises.

1.1

LEVEL
Elementary +

TIME
About 5 minutes

FOCUS
Directing your students' attention and energy to the task at hand

EXTRAS
Variation 2: a reproduction of a painting, a picture of a landscape, a slide projector, a screen, a colour slide of a painting or landscape

FOCUSING

Procedure

1 Ask the students to look at the board, a bare wall, a window, a plant and to concentrate on it.
2 Suggest they close their eyes. Then ask them to imagine a colour they like very much, such as the green of a particular plant they know well, when its first leaves sprout in spring.
3 Observe your class, and when you can sense they are concentrating, gently ask them to picture the classroom in their minds, one element at a time. When they have a complete mental picture of the classroom they can slowly open their eyes.
4 Proceed with the learning activity.

NOTE
The colour you ask your students to visualise influences the direction your students' imagination will take. Dark colours such as black or brown will tend to call up dark scenes or unpleasant memories, colours such as white, yellow, light blue or green will bring back sunny views and warm atmospheres etc. Take this into account when you use this activity as a lead-in for one of the other exercises in this book.

VARIATION 1

1 Ask your students to close their eyes.
2 Ask them to imagine they are in a room they like being in. 'What is the colour of that room? Why do you like being in that particular room?'
3 Ask your students to focus on an essential aspect of the room.
4 Observe your class, and when you can sense they are concentrating, gently ask them to superimpose the picture of that room and the image they have of the classroom. The picture of the room must become vaguer, while the picture of the classroom must become clearer. When they can picture the classroom very clearly they can slowly open their eyes.
5 Proceed with the learning activity.

VARIATION 2

Choose a reproduction of an appropriate painting. Monochrome, near monochrome or abstract paintings facilitate a change of mood.

Good for this purpose are some of the later paintings by Turner, such as: *Sun Setting over a Lake* (Tate Gallery, London NO4665). Many modern paintings by Kandinsky (e.g. *Cossacks*, Tate Gallery, London, NO4948), Hartung (e.g. *Composition T. 51–10*, Royal Museum of Modern Art, Brussels), Pollock (e.g. *Yellow Islands*, Tate Gallery, London, TOO436) work well too.

1 Position the reproduction so that everyone can see it well.
2 Ask your students to concentrate on any part of the painting that strikes them.
3 Ask them to close their eyes and mentally build a pattern around the part they have chosen and so create their own painting, as it were.
4 Observe your class attentively while they do this, and let them go on with their painting until you can tell by the expression on their faces that their mood has changed.
5 Ask your students questions about the mood you can 'read' from their faces. For example, 'What makes you so happy, surprised, puzzled . . . ?' 'Think of a word to describe your mood.' They answer the questions mentally.
6 Then, ask your learners to make a mental picture of the classroom, starting from any element in the painting that has a link with the classroom, and then to open their eyes very slowly.

NOTES

1 You can also use pictures of landscapes.
2 You can also project a slide of a painting or landscape and ask your students to look at the image on the screen. Slowly turn the lens of the projector to obtain a blurred image and proceed as above.

ACKNOWLEDGEMENT
We learnt the technique of bringing everyone back to reality by picturing the classroom in their minds from a seminar at the Kreis-volkshochschule Main-Kinzig, Gelnhausen, Germany. These seminars are derived from the work of Bernard Dufeu at Mainz University.

1.2

LEVEL
Elementary +

TIME
About 5 minutes

FOCUS
Directing your
students' attention

EXTRAS
None

FOLLOW THE SPIRAL

Procedure

1 Draw a top view of a spiral on the board (see Fig. 1). Start in the middle of the board until you reach the sides of the board.
2 Ask your students (who remain seated) to point at the outer end of the spiral and then to follow the spiral slowly with an index finger until they reach the centre of the spiral.
3 Proceed with the lesson.

Fig. 1

VARIATION 1

When your students are used to doing this exercise, you can ask them to draw a spiral on a sheet of paper. Ask them to start from the outer end of the spiral at a point near the edge of the paper, and draw progressively towards the centre of their sheet.

VARIATION 2

Ask your students to *mentally* draw a spiral, starting from the outer end of the spiral. Instruct them to close their eyes and to follow their individual spiral by making circular movements with their heads. When your students reach the centre, their heads stop moving. This is the moment to proceed with your activity.

VARIATION 3

1 Ask your students to close their eyes and imagine they are standing at the mouth of a long round tunnel.
2 They look into it. In the distance the tunnel gradually gets darker and its diameter appears to decrease.
3 All that your students can make out at the end of the tunnel is a point of light. They look at this point.
4 They move to that point and they progressively discern what there is at the end of the tunnel. It is their classroom. When they can see the classroom very clearly, they open their eyes.
5 Go on with your lesson.

VARIATION 4

This is useful to stimulate your students' imagination.
1 Draw a spiral on the board, or project a transparency with a spiral on a screen. Next, ask your students to follow the spiral with their eyes, starting from its centre.
2 Tell them to close their eyes when they reach the outer limit of the spiral and to prolong the spiral mentally.
3 When all eyes are closed, play the music for your main activity and proceed with your lesson.

THIS MUSIC MAKES ME FEEL LIKE . . .

The students need to know the pattern *feel like* + *ing*.

Procedure

1 Start by telling your students they are going to listen to something 'special', specially chosen for that day, and that you want them to tell you what they feel like doing when they hear it.
2 Play the music you have chosen. When your class is concentrating on the music, cut it off abruptly. Invite your students to express what this music makes them feel like doing, whatever it may be. Allow those students who are most willing or eager to talk to do so.
3 As soon as you sense the class is with you, get on with your lesson.

SUGGESTED MUSIC

To energize your students, choose something fast or catchy such as work songs, Negro spirituals (e.g. 'Joshua fit the battle of Jericho').

A lot of ethnic music is appropriate: Celtic dance music from Ireland or Spanish Galicia, for instance, preferably played on the fiddle; Indian ragas using the flute and tabla; and African dance rhythms. German and East European folklore are a mine of tunes. Jazz can also be used here.

Examples

1 India: *Question–Answer* – 'Teen taal' and 'Drut Laya' as played by Ustad Sabir Khan on Nataraj CD NM 004
2 *Les Maîtres Tambours du Burundi (Master Drummers from Burundi)* on Arion ARN 64016
3 *Ach Du lieber Augustin* (Germany)

Some suitable pieces of Western classical music

1 The fast movements in works by Paganini, such as the last movements of his violin concertos
2 Sarasate: *Zigeunerweisen*, Op. 20, Finale
3 Khatchaturian: 'Sabre Dance' and other lively dances from the ballets *Gayaneh* and *Spartacus*
4 Dvořák: *Slavonic Dances* (one of the livelier ones)

To relax your students choose classical music with a slow regular rhythm. Two-minute excerpts are ideal, for example:
1 Paganini: Concertos for Violin and Orchestra, e.g. Nos. 3 and 4, excerpts from the second movement of each concerto
2 Sarasate: *Zigeunerweisen*, Op. 20, the violin solo before the Finale is very suitable
3 Vaughan Williams: Fantasia on 'Greensleeves', Introduction or Finale ('Greensleeves' theme) or middle section ('Lovely Joan' theme)
4 Vieuxtemps: Concerto No. 4 in D minor for Violin and Orchestra, Op. 31, second movement
5 Indian music: an evening raga, such as *Rag Lalit* (e.g. on Nimbus NI 5152, with Hariprasad Chaurasia and Anindo Chatterjee)
6 Vietnamese music: 'Kieu Du Xuan' ('Kieu's Spring Walk'), first part
7 Rodrigo: *Fantasia para un gentilhombre*, second movement

1.3

LEVEL
Elementary +

TIME
5–10 minutes

FOCUS
Helping the learners switch on to the language lesson

EXTRAS
None

1.4

LEVEL
Beginners +;
Elementary + with
nursery rhymes

TIME
5–10 minutes

FOCUS
Energizing the
class and creating
a sense of
togetherness

EXTRAS
None

BEAT THE RHYTHM

Preparation

Choose a piece of music with a clear rhythm.

Procedure

1 Tell your students they are going to listen to music and clap their hands to the rhythm. They remain seated to do this.

2 Play a piece of music with a fairly simple rhythm. (If you use this activity regularly, use pieces with increasingly complex rhythms.) Get the whole class to beat the rhythm with their hands.

 If the students can do this, they are ready to work together in class and you can move on to the language work.

SUGGESTED MUSIC

- Do not try Indian classical music, as the complexity of the rhythms can be awesome, but folk music is often sung and danced with people clapping their hands. Any piece that 'invites' people to do this is appropriate. Circus music often matches this description. Here are some well-known examples of folk music: 'What shall we do with a drunken sailor?', 'This old man', 'She'll be coming round the mountain when she comes', 'We shall not be moved', 'Kalinka'.

- African music played on drums and on the 'thumb piano' (lamellophone), known regionally as sansa, likembe or ubi, is suitable, for example Francis Bebey's *Sassandra* (OMCD 005).

- A lot of nursery rhymes work well, and singing the lyrics while clapping provides a good transition to language work. The lyrics themselves may be the subject of the lesson, for example: 'Old King Cole', 'Humpty Dumpty', 'Hickory dickory dock', 'Pop goes the weasel'.

 The *Oxford Nursery Rhyme Book* (Opie 1955) contains 800 rhymes. Base your choice on the complexity of the rhythm, the pace of the music and the text of the rhyme (i.e. its length, linguistic difficulty and content).

- Fast classical music is suitable too:
 1 Handel: excerpts from *Water Music*. Choose a slower movement to start with, then a faster one
 2 Rossini: 'Galop' from the Overture to *William Tell*
 3 Purcell (attributed): 'Lillibulero'
 4 Ravel: *Boléro*
 5 Mozart: Symphony No. 40 in G minor, K 550, opening of the first movement
 6 'Schiarazula Marazula' (a Renaissance dance)

MUSICAL DIALOGUE

You can also use this activity as an ice-breaker.

Procedure

1 Explain that music is a language, which we have to learn just as we learnt our mother tongue. When we first started speaking, we began with mere sounds, yet we somehow established a kind of communication with the people around us.

2 Tell your students they are going to try to communicate in a similar way today by using their hands only.

3 Clap a simple rhythm with your hands, and invite your students to imitate you, in the same way as a baby trying to imitate someone speaking. Anyone who feels ready to imitate you can do so. After a number of individuals have done this, ask several students to imitate you together. Then get the whole group to do this.

4 Now ask individual students to clap a rhythm of their own. You imitate, and so do the other students.

5 Tell your students they should no longer just echo the original rhythm, but 'answer' it with a rhythm of their own. This is best done as a chain exercise – one student leads, the next student answers, a third student answers the second, and so on, round the group till everyone has had a turn.

 After this musical conversation, your students are ready for linguistic exchanges.

VARIATION

For this you need one or more percussion instruments, e.g. a xylophone, glockenspiel, tambourine, African thumb piano (sansa/likembe), or Indian tablas, bongoes, maracas. You can also use a Jew's harp or any other instrument you have available with which the students can readily produce an acceptable sound.

1 Place one or more instruments in the middle of the classroom.

2 Ask your students to sit in a circle or semicircle around the instrument(s).

3 To give your students confidence, ask them whether they can recognise the instrument(s) and if they can play it/them. If you are not a musician yourself, tell them you yourself cannot play the instrument(s).

4 Proceed as in Steps 1–5 above, but this time instead of hands, use the instrument(s).

5 Ask a student to play the instrument and lead the class. The other students answer with their hands.

6 If you have several instruments, a musical dialogue is initiated by one student playing one instrument and other students answering with the other instruments, while the rest of the class clap their hands. The variations on this are potentially infinite.

7 Encourage your students to lead the class in turns.

1.5

LEVEL
Elementary +

TIME
10 minutes

FOCUS
Improving the dynamic of the group

EXTRAS
For the Variation, a variety of percussion instruments

1.6

LEVEL
Elementary +

TIME
5–10 minutes

FOCUS
Getting the group alert

EXTRAS
None

MOVE TO THE MUSIC

Students must be receptive to an approach involving physical movement before you can think of introducing activities where they move in your class. You may need to prepare your students progressively over the weeks. But even 'serious' adults may welcome the change from the routine of sitting down all the time.

Procedure

1 Tell your students they are going to listen to some music and that everyone in class is going to move their hands and/or their feet to the music, while remaining seated.
2 Play the music (excerpts of about three minutes are enough) and encourage the class by setting an example. Follow the flow of the music with your hand(s) and feet. Make sure your gestures are broad, for students are unlikely to do something you dare not do yourself.
3 When everyone is moving their hands and/or feet as you would like, begin to talk about this music to the class, for example: 'Do you like this music?', 'Do you listen to music when you work/study/eat?', 'What kind of music would you have preferred to listen to?', 'Do you move your hands or feet when you listen to music at home?' . . . or gambits suited to the learners, the music and the moment.

Do not discourage spontaneous exchanges among students. Sometimes strong feelings emerge. When it comes to this, you have undoubtedly achieved your aim.

SUGGESTED MUSIC
Folk music
Catchy music such as folk music from the Andes, Africa, the Caribbean, India and North America.
Some good Western folk tunes:
1 'My bonnie lies over the ocean'
2 'Sur le pont d'Avignon' (France)
3 'The animals went in two by two'
4 'Vi gå över daggstänkta berg' (Sweden)
5 'De zevensprong' (Holland)

Some classical pieces
1 Johann Strauss (elder): *Radetzky March*
2 J.S. Bach: Sonata for Flute and Basso Continuo in E major, BWV 1035, second movement (Allegro)
3 Rossini: Overture to *The Thieving Magpie (La gazza ladra)*, especially the 'crescendo'
4 Verdi: 'Anvil Chorus' from *Il Trovatore*
5 Classical Indian music with tabla (the fast movements)

EXTENSION
Ask your students to actually walk and move to music you have chosen. The size and layout of the class must allow everyone to move easily and,

if necessary, ask the class to move furniture aside. Follow this up with some language work that the students can do standing or seated on desks, or for which they have to move.

Pick music with not too hectic a tempo for the first try, such as Renaissance dance music by Praetorius, Attaignant and many anonymous composers, for example the piece 'Schiarazula Marazula'.

MOVE AS . . .

Preparation

Choose a piece of music suited to the way you want your students to move.

If you want to relax your students, choose slow music. Ask everyone to move as if they are an instrument used in the excerpt such as the violin, guitar, organ, or as if they are playing one of the instruments.

If you want to energize your class, choose a lively piece and ask your students to move as if they are opera stars, conductors, dancers, the bow of a violin, an electric guitar player, etc.

You can also ask them to move as if they are music critics, retired ballerinas, confused dancers, old sailors, etc.

Procedure

1 Explain to your students that music is ideal for inducing movement. Today you would like them to move to music, but in a special way.
2 Ask the class to stand up and to move the furniture if necessary.
3 Explain how you want them to move.
4 Play about two minutes of music and encourage everyone to move. Join in!
5 With beginners or elementary learners, go on to your lesson.
   In more advanced classes, discuss how it feels to move in the way they did.

SUGGESTED MUSIC

The choice is wide. You can use any kind of music: ethnic, jazz, classical and pop. If you would like your students to move as if they are an instrument, choose solo pieces first. Later you can use pieces with several instruments and ask the students to move as if they are different instruments. The results can be fascinating. Here we give a couple of examples only.

To energize
1 'Oh! When the saints go marching in'
2 Arne: 'Rule Britannia'
3 Verdi: 'La donna è mobile' from *Rigoletto*
4 Mozart: *Eine kleine Nachtmusik*, K 525, first and third movements
5 Bizet: 'Toreador' and 'Habañera' from *Carmen*
6 Brahms: Hungarian Dances (one of the livelier ones)

1.7

LEVEL
Elementary +

TIME
5–10 minutes

FOCUS
Energizing or relaxing

EXTRAS
None

REQUIREMENT
The size and layout of the class must allow everyone to move easily

To relax

1 'Greensleeves'
2 Sibelius: *Finlandia* (a quieter section)
3 Mozart: *Eine kleine Nachtmusik,* K 525, second movement
4 Handel: Concerto for Harp and Chamber Orchestra in B flat, second movement (Larghetto)
5 Haydn: Concerto No. 1 in C for Violin and Orchestra, second movement
6 Brahms: Sonata for Violin and Piano No. 2 in A, Op. 100, second movement

1.8

LEVEL
Elementary +

TIME
3–10 minutes

FOCUS
Raising the energy level

EXTRAS
Enough space to dance

DANCE

To do these dances effectively you need at least eight people in the group, including yourself. We are using the anonymous dance 'La morisque' (Susato Collection 1551) to illustrate the dance steps (🔲). We intend it to be so simple that students who 'can't dance' will discover that in fact they can. We find circle dances particularly good as ice-breakers at the beginning of a course and as a way of saying goodbye at the end.

Procedure

1 Clear a space. Tell your class to form an inward-facing circle. Include yourself in the circle. Everyone holds hands with the person on either side.
2 Explain the dance steps as follows:
   • One step per beat throughout.
   • Starting with the left foot, four steps forwards towards the centre of the circle, then four steps back again.
   • Repeat all so far.
   • Turn to the right and take eight steps to the right.
   • Turn to the left and take eight steps to the left.
   • Repeat the entire sequence till the music stops.
3 Now put on the music and dance. If the first time you do the dance is a bit of a shambles, treat it as a 'dress rehearsal' and repeat it as a 'performance'. Then go on to the rest of the lesson.

VARIATION

If someone in your class plays the recorder, get them to play the music instead of listening to the cassette. Get another student to beat the rhythm on a tambourine, drum or desk-top. If none of them plays but you can, use the cassette the first time so that you can lead the dance, but the second time play the recorder while the class dance. The music for the dance, plus a suggested rhythm to beat is given in Fig. 2 opposite.

Fig. 2

EXTENSION

You may find that some of your students are very good dancers or may be having dancing lessons. Ask two or three of them to work together and produce a dance. This may be a simple one for the class to do or a more complex one which they can perform before the others. If they produce a simple one, ask them to explain the steps to the class; if it is more complex, ask them to explain the process they went through to create it. Give them the music or let them choose their own.

ACKNOWLEDGEMENTS

We learnt the idea of using circle dances in class from June McOstrich in a session at the IATEFL conference at Warwick in April 1989. The extension is based on an idea we learnt from Mario Rinvolucri.

1.9 BACKGROUND MUSIC

'I really think it was an excellent idea to improve our classes with music, which I find very important because it makes us more relaxed and able to think.'

'I love your idea of playing classical music during our classes. It both gives us inspiration and helps us to relax.'

These spontaneous comments from our students bring home the two main reasons why we use background music in class, namely that it helps to create a relaxed atmosphere and it helps our students to concentrate. We have used it for the following purposes:

- creating a relaxed atmosphere as our students come into class – those that are already there can listen while we wait for late-comers;
- helping our students to concentrate on written work and making exercises more bearable;
- breaking silence at the beginning of oral work done in pairs and groups – stopping the music is then a good way of bringing the oral work to an end;
- marking a brief pause in the lesson before moving onto another activity;
- ending the lesson as we began.

When you use background music, check two things: firstly, that it is genuinely 'in the background', i.e. not too loud; secondly, that it is not too directional, i.e. strongly directed to part of the room, while in other parts there is too little sound. You can get round this problem by directing the speaker(s) towards a wall so that the sound is reflected into the room.

The choice of music is very important. Other than when the students are leaving class, when you can also use lively music, it needs to be above all relaxing. Vocal music tends to be distracting because of the words. Here are suggestions based on what we have found effective:

1 Music by Baroque composers, especially Vivaldi, Albinoni, J.S. Bach (in particular the lute suites), J.C. Bach, Telemann, Pergolesi (above all, the flute concertos)
2 Music by Mozart, especially the concertos
3 Lute and classical guitar music, especially by Dowland
4 Piano music by Satie, the Nocturnes by Field and rags by Scott Joplin.
5 Harp music, e.g. Celtic and mediaeval music, music by Andreas Vollenweider
6 Indian music: try any morning raga, for example, one performed by Ravi Shankar or Hariprasad Chaurasia and Anindo Chaterjee
7 Music played on the Asian zither, e.g. the Vietnamese dan tranh (sixteen strings) and the Japanese koto (twelve strings)
8 Japanese shakuhachi music

Good Suggestopedic cassettes can be obtained from: SEAL (The Society for Effective Affective Learning), Western Language Centre Ltd., Forge House, Kemble, Glos. GL7 6AD, England.

We have also found that our students appreciate listening to nature sounds in the background. An increasing number are available in commercially produced recordings. We have used the following with success:

- birdsong (a general background of birdsong rather than individual species)
- cicadas and crickets at night
- running water (as from a mountain brook)
- forest sounds
- rain beating down (but without thunder)
- a crackling fire

These are particularly effective with classes in the evening.

CHAPTER 2

Talking about music

Here the activities help you to teach the language needed to talk about music, including identifying, making deductions and comparisons. Activity 2.4 *Conversations about music* provides a framework within which you and your class can listen to and discuss music on a regular basis and tells you the kind of phrases they will need in order to do so.

2.1

LEVEL
Elementary +

TIME
10–15 minutes to practise; up to 30 minutes to teach the target structures

FOCUS
Identifying (*It/This is* . . ., *That was* . . .), recognising instruments, voices and pieces of music

EXTRAS
Dictation (example given) and OHP for Extension 2

IDENTIFYING MUSIC

Preparation

Make two selections of up to five different pieces of music as suggested below.

Procedure

We give musical instruments as examples to show how to proceed, but the procedure can easily be applied to voices and pieces of music too. The sections dealing with music in the *Longman Lexicon* give a good choice of lexis.

1 If necessary teach or revise the names of the instruments in English first. Use pictures or drawings for this.
2 To teach *That was* . . ., proceed as follows. Play a short piece of piano music and say: 'Listen, it's a piano.' Turn off the music and say: 'That was a piano.' Proceed similarly with a recording of another instrument and ask: 'What's this? / What instrument was that?' The students should answer: 'It's a guitar. / That was a guitar', depending on whether the instrument is still playing or not. Encourage your students to combine this with expressions such as *I think/reckon / If you ask me*. If you cannot elicit the wording you want, say it yourself. When you are satisfied everyone has mastered the structures needed, move on to Step 3.
3 Tell your students they are going to hear more short excerpts with instruments to identify. Play the first selection. Ask the class to write down their answers, and then to compare with their neighbours.
4 Repeat Step 3 with a selection of more difficult instruments and divide the class into teams of four to eight. Each group must decide as a team. A team gets one point for each correct guess. The team that has the highest number of correct answers wins.

VARIATION 1

Another way to proceed in Step 3 is to give a random list (written on the board, or dictated) and ask the class to write down or tick the names of the instruments as they hear them.

VARIATION 2

Instead of instruments, get your students to identify pieces of music. Take national anthems, for example. Play the excerpts one by one, identifying each as it is played. Then play the excerpts in a different order and invite the students to identify the passages as in the main activity. In intermediate + classes, ask your students to explain how they recognise the different anthems, e.g. 'I know it's the Italian anthem because it sounds like music from an opera'.

EXTENSION 1

Ask your students to prepare their own sets of selections. Students who do this can lead an activity during another lesson.

EXTENSION 2

Give your students a dictation, the kind where, if they don't know how to spell something, they can ask. See the example passage below. Read the passage right through once, then twice section by section (indicated by /), then once again straight through. When you have finished, project the dictation on an OHP, or if you don't have one, write it on the board. More ideas for dictations with a difference can be found in *Dictation – New Methods, New Possibilities* (Davis and Rinvolucri 1988).

Example text for dictation

An orchestra contains / instruments of various kinds: / the strings, the woodwind, / the brass and the percussion. / The director of an orchestra / is called the conductor. / He keeps the orchestra together / and guides their interpretation / by beating with a baton / and through other gestures. / He reads the music / from an orchestral score. / The members of the orchestra / read their music from parts. / Both the conductor's score / and the players' parts / rest on music stands.

EXTENSION 3

Ask your students to classify instruments in the following categories: woodwind, brass, strings, percussion. Expand, if necessary, by giving some they had not thought of such as: piccolo, cor anglais, bassoon, tuba, French horn, viols, lute, timpani, snare drum, gong, glockenspiel (looks like a xylophone, but is made of metal), etc.

EXTENSION 4

Proceed likewise for voices. In elementary classes ask students to identify different kinds of voices (soprano, bass, etc.). In more advanced classes, introduce the quality of voices (melodious, wheezy, clear, piercing, sonorous, strident, velvety, squeaky, etc.) Students love to bring in their own choices of singers.

SUGGESTED MUSIC

- For beginners and students at elementary level, prepare five excerpts of thirty seconds each of different musical instruments. Having introduced well-known instruments, choose more difficult or exotic ones. Some possible selections:

  1 the violin, piano, guitar, flute, saxophone
  2 the harpsichord, oboe, recorder, lute, cello
  3 the koto (Japanese zither), shakuhachi (Japanese bamboo flute), the shamisen
  4 the (African) thumb piano (sansa or likembe), talking drum, musical bow, whistle, kora, balafon
  5 the Indian tabla, bamboo flute, vina, bells, dhak, sitar, sarod, sarang.

  Next take excerpts of fifteen seconds only.

- Use Britten's *Young Person's Guide to the Orchestra*. This is an interesting listening comprehension exercise as students will hear a commentary introducing them to the sound of each instrument. Prokofiev's *Peter and the Wolf* can also be used for one-by-one introduction of instruments.

- If you choose national anthems, select some that are easy to recognise first. In Europe we would recommend the British, Dutch, French, German, and Italian anthems. Another selection of easily recognisable anthems would be the American, Chinese, Japanese and Finnish ones.

  Next, take anthems of which the tunes are less easy to distinguish, such as the Austrian, Belgian, Danish, Luxembourg and Swiss anthems.

  Recordings of national anthems are easily available. If you can play an instrument you can find the scores in *Nationalhymnen* (Institut für Auslandsbeziehungen 1970).

- You can also choose excerpts from operas (by Mozart, Wagner, Verdi, Offenbach and Mussorgsky, for instance) or other kinds of music that you know will be stimulating and challenging for your students.

DEGREES OF CERTAINTY

When people listen to music they don't know, they often try to guess what it is, who wrote it, when it was written and so on. In this activity we exploit this natural tendency in order to practise or teach modal verbs. Your students need to have learnt adjectives of nationality beforehand. If you use this activity as an initial presentation of modal verbs used for deduction, follow Variation 1.

Preparation

Prepare a selection of, ideally, five excerpts of music from different countries. You can make this more fun by choosing misleading pieces such as those suggested at the end of this activity. If you are using a slide projector, check that it is completely *out* of focus.

Procedure

1 Project a slide so out of focus that you get very little idea of what it shows. Ask your students to speculate what it is. Encourage them to use expressions with modal verbs, i.e. *It may/might/could be* .... While gradually sharpening the focus, encourage speculation until some students have a fairly clear, if not exact, idea of what it is. At this point encourage those who think they have some specific clue to use *It must be* .... Ask them to justify their guess. Ask those that have some objection to a guess to counter it with *It can't be* ..., plus a reason. Show the slide in focus so that everyone can see what it really *is* a picture of. Repeat this whole process with two or three more slides.

   If you don't have a slide projector, choose a picture from a book. Go round your class showing the picture for a moment to one group, then another, then another till all have seen it – but make sure they see it so momentarily that they only get the slightest idea as to what is in the picture. Follow the same process as with the slide projector and encourage your students to speculate about the picture using the three target modal verbs. Replicate the effect of gradually sharpening focus by flashing the picture for a little longer each time after speculations have ceased to flow.

2 Write this table on the board:

Certain	It is . . . (if you know)
	It must be . . . (if you have at least one piece of evidence and so are speculating)
Uncertain	It could be . . .
	It may be . . .
	It might be . . .
Certainly not	It can't be . . . (if you are speculating)
	It isn't . . . (if you know)

2.2

LEVEL
Intermediate +

TIME
15 minutes to practise; 30 minutes to teach

FOCUS
Modal verbs expressing deduction; Expressing certainty as opinion (Variation 4); Speaking; Writing

EXTRAS
Slide projector, if available, and 3–4 slides. Otherwise, a book with pictures in it. For Variation 1, pictures of people in national and 'international' dress

3 Tell your students you are going to play them a series of short excerpts of music from different countries. Ask them to write the name of the country they think it is from and the word *certain* or *uncertain* beside it, according to how sure they are. Play the excerpts.

4 Point to the table on the board. Tell them to write a sentence about the nationality of each excerpt using *could be, may be* or *might be* if they are uncertain, *must be* if they are certain but don't know the music, *is* if they know the music. Ask them to tell you their sentences. If anyone disagrees with a *must be* sentence, encourage them to challenge it with a *can't be* sentence with the inclusion of a reason.

VARIATION 1

If you are giving an initial presentation of modal verbs for deduction, then start as follows:

Find three pictures of people in 'international costume', i.e. clothes that might be worn in any country. Find four more pictures of people in clearly identifiable national costumes, e.g. a Scotsman in a kilt, a Greek man in traditional dress, a cowboy, a Japanese woman in a kimono, a Dutch lady with a lace bonnet, the national costume where you are teaching.

1 Show a picture of someone wearing clothes that might be worn almost anywhere, e.g. a man in a suit, a woman wearing a stylish blouse and skirt, a young person in blue jeans and a T-shirt. Ask your class, 'Where do you think s/he is from? England?' Let them answer, then ask, 'Are you certain?' They won't be, so add, 'Well, s/he could be from England.' Get everyone to repeat. Check for oral accuracy. Show another picture of someone else in 'international costume'. Repeat the process. This time introduce *could, may* and *might* as alternatives to one another. Repeat this process a third time to reinforce the point.

2 Then show a picture of someone in national dress, where it is clear where the person must be from. Elicit the nationality. Ask them how they know, then add, 'Because of . . . s/he must be (nationality).' Do the same with a second picture but deliberately tell your students that the person is of a different nationality from what s/he really is. Get them to disagree with you, using 'She can't be (nationality) because . . .'. Elicit a *must be* sentence for another picture and a *can't be* sentence for another. Don't forget to check that everyone has got the sounds and words right and is clear about the meaning.

3 Do the main activity starting at Step 1.

VARIATION 2

Instead of speculating about nationality, they can guess the instrument that is being played (in which case they need to know the names of instruments). Revise the names of instruments first, if necessary.

VARIATION 3

Instead of speculating about nationality, they can guess when the music was written (in which case they need to know expressions such as *in the mid-eighteenth century, mediaeval/contemporary music*) or they can guess who wrote it. In either case they need the modal perfect forms *must have written, could have written*, etc. As a lead into this, in Step 1 switch off the slide projector or lay the book down on the table to mark the fact that you are now dealing with the past. Then start the speculation work but with *could/may/might have been* and continue to use modal perfect forms.

VARIATION 4

Instead of using modal verbs people often express degrees of certainty by giving opinions. To practise this, you can do any of the above activities but using the following, or similar, exponents:

Degrees of certainty (expressed as opinion)

Very probable	I am sure it is . . .
	I am certain it is . . .
	I think it is . . .
Unclear	I suspect it is . . .
	I've an idea it might be . . .
Very improbable	I am not sure it is . . .
	I am not certain it is . . .
	I don't think it is . . .
	I (honestly) doubt it is . . .

SUGGESTED MUSIC

Choose any music that is not too obvious, so that there will be some guesswork involved. You may also choose deliberately misleading music, such as excerpts from:

1 Bizet: *L'Arlésienne, Carmen*. They sound Spanish, but Bizet was French.
2 Borodin: *Polovtsian Dances*. They sound Asian, but Borodin was Russian.
3 Copland: *Billy the Kid*. This sounds like film music; Copland was American.
4 Kabalevsky: *Cello Concerto No. 2*, an excerpt from the second movement, which includes a number of fascinating sounds.
5 Lehár: *The Land of Smiles (Das Land des Lächelns)*. Parts of it sound Chinese, but Lehár was Austrian.

2.3

LEVEL
Intermediate +

TIME
15–30 minutes or
even more,
depending on the
level of
comparison

FOCUS
Comparing and
describing musical
genres, musical
styles and
interpretations;
Speaking;
Developing
appreciation of
music

EXTRAS
None

COMPARING MUSIC

Your students need to know how to make comparisons in English.

Preparation

Prepare a selection of short pieces of music (three is ideal).

Procedure

1 Tell your students they are going to compare the excerpts they are going to hear.
2 Play your selection. A grid such as the one in Fig. 3 below – adapted to the music chosen – helps to focus the students' attention on particular aspects.

  In more advanced classes discuss the points to concentrate on with the students, and draw up a listening grid with their help.

	1	2	3
Voice			
Interpretation			
Arrangement			
Speed			
Instruments			

Fig. 3

Here are some more aspects they can take into consideration:

a Music Any music can be described in relation to its purpose, voices/instruments, rhythm, harmony and melody. The following questions also stimulate the students:
Does the instrumentation differ?
Is the style the same?
Are they equally energetic?

b Genres Folk, blues, heavy metal, electronic, rock, classical, mediaeval, opera, folk dance, pop, Negro spiritual, bagpipe, church

c Performance
Are the instruments modern or period?
Is there a difference in the style of playing/singing?
Are they all equally expressive?
Are they equally good in terms of technique?
Are the interpretations equally satisfactory?

Be prepared to give your students the vocabulary they may need or put some information source such as the *Longman Lexicon* at their disposal. (Note that Activity 2.1 *Identifying music* deals with this kind of vocabulary.)

3 To speak about the music your students will of course identify the pieces, instrument etc. After comparing, it is very natural to express likes and dislikes, to state preferences and to give the reasons for all this.

SUGGESTED MUSIC

Any music with elements to compare is suitable. Select pieces of two to three minutes.

1 Compare arrangements of the same music for different instruments (e.g. piano, guitar, lute). For example compare excerpts from Mussorgsky's *Pictures at an Exhibition* in the piano version with the version orchestrated by Ravel.
2 Compare excerpts from works directed by different conductors, or played or sung by different interpreters. Christmas songs provide easily available material for this.
3 Compare musical renderings of feelings and scenes across cultures. For instance Japanese, Chinese or Vietnamese music describing the spring, 'Spring' from Vivaldi's 'Four Seasons' or Paganini's 'La primavera'. African and European church music provide striking contrasts too.

CONVERSATIONS ABOUT MUSIC

2.4

For many people a love of music of one kind or another is a vital part of their life. This activity provides a framework for sharing that love of music. Use any music that you enjoy and that you would like others to hear.

LEVEL
Lower intermediate +

Procedure

TIME
20 minutes +

1 Tell your students they are going to listen to some music and you would like their reactions to it.
2 Ask them what kind of expressions they think they will need to talk about the music (e.g. ways of expressing likes and dislikes). Elicit examples that they already know and add further expressions according to your students' level. If you think they are appropriate, include the expressions below – they have all arisen in our lessons.

FOCUS
Talking about musical likes/dislikes; Describing music

EXTRAS
None

Likes and dislikes
I can't say that I like it.
It doesn't do anything for me.
I find it . . .
I'm not used to listening to this kind of music.
It's the kind of music you can grow/learn to like/appreciate.

Reacting to music:

It's		boring.
		exciting.
I find this music		relaxing.
		restful.
This piece	is	sumptuous.
passage		repetitive.
excerpt		monotonous.
movement		sensuous.
		sad.

Recognising music

X is one of my favourite singers/composers.
Whenever I hear this . . .

Forming associations

When I hear this I think of . . .
It reminds me of . . .

Sometimes students want to refer to a particular point in the music and want to use expressions such as:

The bit that goes . . .
. . . where the music gets faster/slower/louder/softer . . .

When they talk about the physical quality of sounds, the students often need these words and phrases:

loud
soft/(quiet)   } volume

high/top notes
low/bottom notes   } pitch

sharp (above the note)
flat (below the note) } tuning
out-of-tune

3 Play the music.

4 Ask your students for their reactions. Chair a discussion. As they talk, write on slips of paper anything they say that you wish to draw attention to (one per slip of paper) – these may be errors or good turns of phrase they have said.

5 Optionally, repeat Steps 3 and 4 with one or more further pieces of music.

6 Divide the class into groups. Divide the slips of paper equally among the groups. Ask each group to decide which slips contain errors and which good phrases. Tell them to correct the errors.

7 Discuss the good phrases, the errors and their corrections with the class.

VARIATION 1

Instead of preteaching the items in Step 2, you can let these expressions arise spontaneously in Step 4, helping your students as the need arises.

VARIATION 2

Ask one or more students to supply the music. This can become a regular feature of your classes, with different students bringing the music on different occasions.

ACKNOWLEDGEMENT

Thanks to Carolina, Isabel, Madalena, Marta, Pedro, Rita, Susana and Teresa for suggesting music as a good topic to talk about in class and for using the expressions that have found their way into this activity.

CHAPTER 3

Grammar

In this chapter your students are asked to listen to music which acts as a stimulus to use a structure they have been practising. In responding to the music they are engaged at a deeper and more personal level than is usually possible with other kinds of practice activity. Consequently, they internalise the structure more fully. Concentration or relaxation tasks are an essential part of most of these activities.

3.1

LEVEL
Intermediate +

TIME
20 minutes

FOCUS
Any tense; Asking questions

EXTRAS
A class set plus two of your questionnaire

MUSICAL QUESTIONNAIRES

The size and layout of the classroom must make it possible for everyone to move about easily. This activity has an energizing effect on the class if done briskly.

Preparation

1 Decide what grammar points your students need to practise, and integrate them into a music questionnaire (see Fig. 4 for examples of questionnaires).
2 Prepare a class set plus two of your questionnaire.
3 Bring in some ten minutes of energetic background music.

Procedure

1 If necessary, explain any vocabulary that may cause problems for your students.
2 Explain to your students that you expect them all to stand up and to go and ask questions to their classmates *one by one*. Ask them to write down the name of the person(s) who answer(s) 'yes' to the questions. Tell them the aim is to get as many answers as possible in the shortest time possible.
3 Get the students to stand up and possibly to move some of the furniture.
4 Hand out the questionnaire, give the 'start' signal and start the music.
5 Provide an example by joining in. Quickly go to a student and ask the questions in the questionnaire. Encourage everyone to keep a brisk pace, e.g. by giving a 'five-minute warning' five minutes before you want them to finish.
6 Stop after ten minutes *at most*. Ask everyone to sit down.
7 Appoint a secretary. In a plenary, proceed question by question to establish who found 'yes' answers. For each question the secretary

writes down the names or initials *not* of the people who said 'yes', but of the people who collected 'yes' answers.

8 Ask the secretary to say who found most names. The secretary also gives a summary report, e.g.:

Most students found someone who listens to music before going to bed, but nobody found someone who sings in the loo. Only half of the class found someone who sings on his/her way to school, etc.

EXTENSION
Encourage your students to write questionnaires of their own and to organise a *Find someone who* . . . activity in a later lesson.

ACKNOWLEDGEMENT
We learnt to use questionnaires for structure practice during a workshop with Mario Rinvolucri at the British Council, Brussels. The basic idea comes from Moskowitz (1978).

Examples of questionnaires

1 The present simple

Find someone who . . .

1	never sings while washing.
2	sings to herself/himself on the way to school/work.
3	usually sings in the loo.
4	hates music during meals.
5	hums to herself/himself when feeling nervous.
6	sings in church on Sundays.
7	plays the guitar.
8	does not like music in general.
9	doesn't listen to his/her favourite music while driving.
10	prefers Mozart to Vivaldi.
11	cannot stand Walkmans in buses and trains.
12	can't stand people singing while they work.
13	can't live without music.
14	sometimes scratches records.
15	doesn't like Italian music.
16	sometimes listens to operas.
17	has a relative who plays an instrument.
18	needs music to go to sleep.
19	borrows records.
20	sings from door to door at Christmas.

Fig. 4

2 Mixed tenses

Find someone who . . .

1 .... has never been to a concert.
2 .... is going to a concert soon.
3 .... used to sing in a choir.
4 .... sings serenades to her boyfriend/his girlfriend.
5 .... went to a concert last month.
6 .... has already been to the opera.
7 .... wishes he/she was a musician.
8 .... is going to buy a CD.
9 .... is saving to buy an instrument.
10 .... has no cassette player.
11 .... is learning to play an instrument.
12 .... has just bought a record, cassette or CD.
13 .... would like to become a pop singer.
14 .... can whistle the national anthem.
15 .... has never been to a dance.
16 .... used to be lulled to sleep with music.
17 .... has already played music in the Underground or in the streets.
18 .... would like to play music for TV.
19 .... will encourage his/her children to learn to play an instrument.
20 .... likes the same music as his/her parents.

© Longman Group UK Ltd. 1992

Fig. 4 cont.

3.2

LEVEL
Intermediate +

TIME
20–30 minutes

FOCUS
The present/past continuous and simple

EXTRAS
None

WHEN I LISTEN(ED) I SEE/SAW . . .

This activity encourages your students to use their imagination.

Preparation

Select a couple of short excerpts (one to two minutes each) that suggest some kind of action.

Procedure

1 Tell your students they are going to translate musical descriptions into English.
2 Help your students to concentrate by doing one of the activities in Chapter 1; Activity 1.1 *Focusing* is suitable. Ask them not to open their eyes before they have listened to the music all the way through. Also, while they listen, they write with their eyes closed. Advise them to

write in a larger hand than usual. Tell them you only want them to write single words, not phrases or sentences.

3 Play the music and as it is playing, quietly ask questions such as: 'Where is it?', 'When?', 'What time?', 'How many people are there?', 'What's happening?'. The students write words, as ideas, images, etc. come to them. When the music has stopped, tell them to slowly open their eyes.

4 Put the students in pairs and ask them to tell each other what they can hear / see happening when they listen to the music, using the words on their sheets as prompts. Ask them to start with the words 'When I listen to this music, I can see . . .'. Monitor and correct.

5 Ask your students to change partners so as to hear another interpretation and to improve their rendition of their thoughts.

6 Invite them to tell their interpretation to the whole class.

7 Repeat Steps 1–6 with another excerpt, but this time, when they exchange their interpretations, they must start with 'When I listened, I saw . . .' Point out the difference between the use of the two tenses. Stress that it is a matter of choice, but that they have to be consistent in their choice.

EXTENSION 1

In a later lesson, follow Steps 1–3 as above, but instead of Step 4, the students in pairs exchange their sheets and, with the help of the cues they have written, they try to describe what their partner sees/saw.

EXTENSION 2

Encourage your students to bring their own music and lead an activity during a later lesson.

EXTENSION 3

Composition: 'When I listen to my favourite music.' Insist they should listen to their favourite music first, with their eyes closed, and write down words to remind them of what they see, etc.

SUGGESTED MUSIC

Film music is very appropriate here, not only music specially composed for a particular film, but also classical music used as film music.

Film music

1 Elmer Bernstein: *The Magnificent Seven / The Return of the Seven*, 'Battle'
2 *Full Metal Jacket*: 'Transition', 'Ruins', 'Leonard', 'Attack', 'Time suspended', 'Sniper'
3 John Williams: Music for *Raiders of the Lost Ark*
4 John Scott: Music for *Greystoke, the Legend of Tarzan, Lord of the Apes*, 'Catastrophe', 'Pygmy Attack', 'Edge of the World', 'Dance of Death', etc.

Classical pieces

1 Walton: 'Passacaglia: Death of Falstaff' from 'Henry V Suite'
2 Saint-Saëns: *Le Rouet d'Omphale*, Finale (Enslavement of Hercules, and Submission)

3 Vaughan Williams: *Sinfonia Antartica*, fifth movement. Choose the excerpt with drums, wind, choir, trumpet, etc.

4 Grieg: Incidental music to *Peer Gynt*, e.g. 'Peer Gynt Hunted by the Trolls', 'Peer Gynt with the Hunchbacks', 'Peer Gynt's Journey Home'

5 Varèse: an excerpt from *Ionisation*

6 Mozart: Piano Concerto No. 21 in C, K 467 (used in many films of which Bo Widerberg's *Elvira Madigan* is maybe the most famous)

Examples of students' work (uncorrected)

When I listen to this music, I see the sea, a boat; it's my boat. The sun is shining. I dive. There are fishes with different colours. It's wonderful. There are also beautiful corals. Two dolphins play with me. It's time. I must go away. I return to the boat. The sun is going down. On the horizon I see a group of dolphins. It's wonderful.

(Christelle, 18)

When I listen to my favourite music I think of the joy of travelling. I imagine myself in a station. I am waiting for a train, but I do not know which train. I will take the first train that arrives.

The sun is shining, it's very hot. I wear shorts, a T-shirt and sportshoes. All I have is a rucksack. I am going to live a long adventure. I do not know where I am going. I get on the train. There are only few people on it. After three hours I finally get off the train. I am in Germany but I do not know the name of the city I am in. I do not understand German. This adds value to my adventure.

I have to find a place to sleep and something to eat, but first I am going to ask for the main touristic points of the area. I hope to find something interesting.

(Sonia, 19)

I like some different kinds of music, pop music, rhythmic music, sad music. Then I react in different ways according to the music I am listening to.

Sometimes music simply makes me happy and sometimes it helps me to concentrate (calm or classical music, of course!).

Music can be a source of sadness too, but sadness can be a kind of satisfaction in certain cases; that's why I sometimes choose to listen to sad music because I am sad and I think it helps to chase this sadness away.

I adore music which transports something magical and captivating, wonderful music of songs which complete each other and imbue me.

Hearing that I feel extremely good. I think about my friends, I imagine a feast with a lot of them around a fire or in a large room with good music only and the one which is making me dream at that moment, of course.

Now and then I put on sweet music to fall asleep. It's very agreeable to be rocked with nice songs: it gives an incredible feeling of well-being.

It's already eleven o'clock. I am going to put on a little beautiful music before going to bed because tomorrow is Friday and I have to wake up at six o'clock. Good night!

(Claude, 18)

FAIRIES

This activity is intended as a free-stage activity after presentation and practice of the present continuous. We demonstrate the technique, using the 'Dance of the Sugar Plum Fairy' from Tchaikovsky's *Nutcracker Suite*. If you are teaching adolescents, who are liable to be silly when talking about fairies, it may be better to build the activity around one of our other suggestions.

Procedure

1 Tell your students you are thinking of something. Add that you are going to tell them about it, but only bit by bit. In response to your hints they must guess what it is. (What you are thinking of is 'fairies'.) Give them the following sentences one at a time, eliciting guesses after each clue.

They're like people but aren't.
They're female.
They don't really exist.
They have wings.
They do magic.
You find them in children's stories.

By now your students will know what you mean but probably won't know the word, so tell them you were thinking of fairies. Write the word *fairy* on the board.

2 Tell the class you are going to play them a piece of music that describes a fairy. Ask them to listen to the music and try to decide where the fairy is and what she's doing. Tell them that if they don't know how to say what they want to in English, they can mime it to you afterwards. Alternatively, if available, they can use bilingual dictionaries. You may want to guide them by writing this frame on the board.

I think she's on/in/at _____ and she's _____ing.

3 Play the music.
4 Give your students any help they need to say what they heard. Put them into pairs and ask them to tell their partner what they heard. Then ask each student to report what their partner heard to the whole class.

   Some people hear the fairy as being in the garden or in a field, dancing; others hear her indoors, especially in the kitchen, doing housework, cleaning with her magic wand, jumping from cake to cake. A few hear a number of actions in the course of the music, particularly a fall or interruption in the middle. We've heard many other interpretations too.

OTHER SUGGESTED MUSIC

Describing fairies
1 Grieg: 'Elfin Dance' from 'Lyric Pieces', Op. 12
2 Mendelssohn: Scherzo from *A Midsummer Night's Dream*

3.3

LEVEL
Elementary

TIME
15–25 minutes

FOCUS
Present continuous; Speaking

EXTRAS
None

Describing other scenes with actions in progress

Bear in mind that you need to adapt according to vocabulary needs.

1 Prokofiev: 'Troika' from *Lieutenant Kijé Suite* (this describes a sleigh-ride across the snow)

2 R. Strauss: *Don Quixote*, Variation Two (this describes Don Quixote's battle against a flock of sheep) or Variation Seven (this describes him flying on what he believes is a winged horse)

3.4

LEVEL
Elementary +

TIME
10–20 minutes

FOCUS
The simple past and *used to*;
Listening; Speaking

EXTRAS
None

CHILDHOOD MEMORIES

Preparation

Choose a piece of music (about two minutes) that personally appeals to you and calls back happy childhood memories.

Procedure

1 Introduce the activity by telling your students that some composers have written nostalgic music evoking memories of their childhood. Tell them they too are going to recall *happy* memories of their own childhood with the help of a piece of music. Ask them to go and sit with a partner of their choice or to sit down in groups of four (depending on the size of the class, the layout of the class and relations between students in the group).

2 Ask the class to close their eyes and to imagine themselves at the age of eighteen, then at the age of twelve, and, finally at the age of seven.

3 Tell your students the music they are going to hear suits the mood of a happy day in their childhood. Play the music softly. Speak quietly and slowly and say something like:

   'Put yourself into the picture you hear. Can you see yourself? Can you feel the atmosphere? You were very happy. What time of the year was it? How late? Was there someone with you? Why were you so happy?'

4 After the music has stopped, ask them to picture the classroom in their minds and slowly open their eyes. They then recount their recollections to their partner(s).

5 Ask them to go on to tell each other things they used to do, like, etc. when they were children.

SUGGESTED MUSIC

1 Bizet: *Jeux d'enfants*

2 Brahms: *Lullaby (Wiegenlied)*, Op. 49 No. 4

3 Debussy:
   a) *Jeux*
   b) *Children's Corner*

4 Elgar:
   a) *Wand of Youth Suite No. 1*
   b) *Wand of Youth Suite No. 2*
   c) *Nursery Suite*
5 Fauré: *Dolly Suite*
6 Mozart: *Lullaby*
7 Ravel: *Mother Goose (Ma mère l'oye)*

MEMORIES OF THINGS PAST

Preparation

Choose three or four short pieces of music (not longer than two minutes each) that personally appeal to you and strongly evoke old memories.

Procedure

1 Start off with a concentration exercise, perhaps Activity 1.2 *Follow the Spiral* (Variation 4, page 10).
2 Play the music you have chosen while your students sit with their eyes closed. Speak calmly and quietly, just loud enough to be understood:
   'Listen to the music, you can see a good moment in your past. Where was it? What kind of day was it? What time of the year? What time of the day? How did you feel? What was the cause of your feelings? Describe the place. Who was there? What happened? What kind of things were important in your life at that time?' etc.
3 Remain silent for fifteen seconds while the music continues. Wait a couple of seconds after the music has stopped and ask your students to progressively picture the classroom in their minds and slowly open their eyes.
4 Ask your students to talk to a partner of their choice about the memories that came back to them. If they wish, they can choose a second partner to talk once more about this.

EXTENSION
Students write a composition about 'Memories of things past . . . '.

SUGGESTED MUSIC
Impressionistic music is best for this, such as piano music by Debussy (e.g. *Préludes, Images*), Ravel (e.g. *Miroirs, Le Tombeau de Couperin*), Fauré (e.g. *Impromptu*, Op. 86)

3.5

LEVEL
Intermediate +

TIME
About 15 minutes

FOCUS
The simple past;
Speaking; Listening

EXTRAS
None

3.6

LEVEL
Intermediate +

TIME
10–15 minutes

FOCUS
The present
perfect with *just*;
Active and passive;
The *going to* future;
The four main
skills

EXTRAS
Optional for the
film music: a video
of the film passage
for your selection

WHAT HAS HAPPENED? . . . IS GOING TO HAPPEN?

This is an excellent activity for all-round stimulation of the imagination.
We exemplify this technique with the present perfect.

Preparation

This activity can be used to practise the present perfect or the *going to*
future. All you need to do is choose very short excerpts of music (about
one minute and even less) that suggest something has happened or is
going to happen, and ask your students to imagine accordingly.

Procedure

1 Get your students to concentrate using Activity 1.2 *Follow the spiral*
(Variation 4, page 10). Ask them to close their eyes.
2 Tell your students you are going to play some music that suggests
something has just happened. Add that they will have to guess what.
3 When you sense the concentration level is right, play an excerpt and
encourage your students to exchange their views as to what happened with a partner.
4 Ask everyone to summarise, orally or in writing, what their partner
has told them – in one sentence. This sentence will follow one of the
patterns which, if necessary, you can write on the board:

Active
Subject + *has/have just* + past participle

Passive
Subject + *has/have just* + *been* + past participle

Monitor and correct where necessary.
If you think it necessary, elicit the reason for using the present
perfect.
5 Then, tell your students to exchange the one-sentence summary with
another partner.
6 Ask your students to repeat Steps 3–6 with another student. This can
be repeated several times.
7 Ask your students each to write their one-sentence summary on the
board – quickly. Allow a few minutes for the class to read these
sentences. Accept any reaction, and encourage the class to correct
where necessary.

EXTENSION 1
If you have taken music from a film, you can show the relevant part from
the film after this. This leads to interesting exchanges.

EXTENSION 2
Students enjoy finding music and leading an activity like this. Encourage
them to bring music in class to try out on one another.

SUGGESTED MUSIC

The present perfect

A lot of film music works well, especially music from thrillers and action films. Some appropriate classical music:

1 R. Strauss: *Also sprach Zarathustra*, opening
2 Nielsen: Symphony No. 5, an excerpt from the end of the second movement where the drums and clarinet play
3 Liszt: *A Faust Symphony*, first part: *Faust*. Quite a few passages work well.
4 Saint-Saëns: Symphony No. 3 ('Organ'. Symphony), opening of the fourth movement
5 Berlioz: *Symphonie Fantastique*, last section of the fourth movement ('March to the Scaffold')

The *going to* future

Any appropriate film music. Thrillers often have music that announces imminent drama. Adapt your choice to the interests of your students.

Some classical music that suggests something is going to happen

1 Berlioz: *Symphonie Fantastique*, last section of the fourth movement ('March to the Scaffold')
2 Beethoven: Symphony No. 5, opening
3 Beethoven: the *Coriolan Overture*, Op. 62, opening
4 Verdi: *Un ballo in maschera* (*A Masked Ball*), opening of Act I, Scene 2
5 R. Strauss: *Till Eulenspiegel,* the passage that announces Till's execution

MY FUTURE/MY PAST IN MUSIC

3.7

LEVEL
Intermediate +

TIME
20–30 minutes

FOCUS
Speaking about the future/past

EXTRAS
None

This activity may bring out very personal feelings. Reserve this for a group of people who know each other well. Do not try this activity if you know someone in the group has been depressed recently. Be prepared to give more time if you find your students have a lot to say.

Preparation

1 Decide if you are going to deal with the past or the future.
2 Select three musical excerpts, each lasting about two minutes, that can evoke a state of mind.

Procedure

1 Tell your class they are going to speak about how they view their own future/past. They are going to hear three short excerpts of music and you expect them to say which one best corresponds to their view of their future/past.

2 Make sure your students are seated comfortably. Help them to concentrate. Our warmer Activity 1.2 *Follow the spiral* (Variation 4, page 10) is best here.

3 Play the three excerpts.

4 Ask your students to work with a partner of their choice. Tell them to say which of the musical excerpts best expresses their view of their future/past and why. As an option, students can explain why the music does not give them a feeling of their future/past, and they attempt to describe what kind of music they feel would be suitable.

EXTENSION

Volunteers bring in music that they feel depicts their future/past. The class can ask them twenty questions to which the answer must be 'yes' or 'no'.

VARIATION

Use one excerpt only. Ask your students to describe the composer's view of his future/past, as suggested by his music. You can then hand out a text in which the composer's mood is described.

SUGGESTED MUSIC

Select three musical excerpts (about two minutes each) that each reflect a different mood. Do not choose too dark a piece. Here are two selections for the main activity and one for the variation.

Selection 1

1 Mozart: Piano Concerto No. 21 in C, K 467, an excerpt from the second movement
2 Nielsen: Clarinet Concerto, first minute
3 Delius: 'Prelude' from *Irmelin*, first minute

Selection 2

1 Nielsen: Symphony No 6, opening of the first movement
2 Nielsen: Symphony No 6, opening of the second movement ('Humoreske')
3 Mozart: Flute Concerto No 1, K 313, opening of the first movement

Selection for the variation

1 Beethoven: Symphony No 3 ('Eroica'), second movement
2 Mozart: Divertimento in F, K 138, second movement
3 Purcell: Chacony in G minor
4 J.S. Bach: Brandenburg Concerto No 2 in F, first movement

SWANS

Students often have a very poor knowledge of names of birds, but we find that they are very keen to know them. For this activity you need two different pieces of music describing a swan.

Procedure

1 Tell your class that the lesson is going to be about birds. Ask them for the names of different parts of a bird. Write them on the board. Your list should include: *wing*, *leg*, *foot*, *crest*, *head*, *beak*, *neck*, *breast* and *tail*. Make sure they also know the term *webbed feet* for ducks, etc.

2 Ask your students to give you the names of birds they have heard of. Write these on the board but tell them not to write in their notebooks yet. They probably won't know many names but will want to know how to say a lot more. For any they want to know, ask them to describe the bird orally to the others in the class, using the vocabulary from Step 1. Encourage the other students to supply the name, otherwise you do so. If you have a bird book available, use it to help identify which bird the student is describing.

   Add these names to the list on the board, plus a few more to extend their vocabulary a little. Make sure that *swan* is on the list.

3 Tell your students to work alone for a moment and to select twelve of the birds listed on the board and write them down in rank order from the one they like most to the one they like least.

4 Elicit from the class or supply, as needed, ways of expressing preferences. Be sure to include: 'I like X most/least.' 'I like X more/less than Y.'   'My favourite/least favourite is. . .'
   Tell your students to work in pairs and tell each other about their preferences. At intermediate and advanced levels, tell them to try and explain why they have these preferences.

5 Show them a picture of a swan, e.g. from your bird book. Ask them to identify and describe it. Ask each student to write down three words describing a swan's *character* (not appearance). When they are ready, ask them for their words and write them on the board.

6 Tell the class they are going to listen to two pieces of music that describe a swan. Ask them to decide afterwards which they prefer and why. Play the two pieces.

7 Put your students into groups of four and ask them to discuss their preferences. After a few minutes of group discussion, chair a class discussion to see if there was any kind of agreement.

VARIATION
In Step 4 you can also practise the structure *I don't like X as much as Y.*

SUGGESTED MUSIC
1 Saint-Saëns: 'The Swan' from *The Carnival of the Animals*
2 Sibelius: *The Swan of Tuonela*, opening two or three minutes
3 Tchaikovsky: Swan theme from the opening of *Swan Lake*, Act II

3.8

LEVEL
Elementary +

TIME
30–45 minutes

FOCUS
Comparatives and superlatives;
Expressing preferences;
Vocabulary relating to birds;
Discussion

EXTRAS
If possible, a book with pictures of birds

CHAPTER 4

Narrative

In the first two activities of this chapter the music will stimulate your students to write imaginative narrative. Activities 4.3 and 4.4 are two exploitations of Prokofiev's musical tale *Peter and the Wolf* and provide a good example of how the same text (and music) can be exploited according to the level and age of the students. Activity 4.5 *Instant drama* takes a musical starting point and leads to a narrative in the form of an improvised drama.

4.1

LEVEL
Intermediate +

TIME
45–90 minutes

FOCUS
Writing

EXTRAS
None

PROMPTING A STORY

Different types of story have different character, plot and stylistic conventions. This activity draws attention to these differences and provides an opportunity to practise the different types.

Procedure

1 Tell your students you are going to work with them on a number of different types of story, namely detective stories, science fiction, love or romantic stories and fairy stories. Divide the class into four groups and assign one story type to each group. Subdivide each group into pairs or threes and ask them to draw up a list of the features typical of their story type. Remind them to deal with typical protagonists, locations, events, atmosphere, endings and deeper meanings or morals. Allow up to ten minutes for this.

2 Write four columns on the board and head them with the story types. Tell your students to do the same. Ask the detective-story group what features they felt were typical of detective stories. Ask first one pair/ three for a feature, then another pair/three, and so on. Write these features on the board. Do the same for the other three story types and groups. The features may include the following:

detective stories – a detective, the detective's assistant, police (often incompetent compared with the detective), a crime (preferably a murder), suspense, attempts to kill the detective, shooting, goodies versus baddies, the villain getting caught;

science fiction – spaceships, aliens, a hero (and heroine), battles, good versus evil, strange planets and stars, suspense;

love stories – a man/boy and a woman/girl in love, an impediment to their happiness, e.g. she's from a rich family and he's from a poor one, events to take them apart, a happy (sometimes tragic) ending; escapism;

fairy stories – fantasy characters such as princes, princesses, giants, animals that talk, fairies, fairy godmothers, witches, stepmothers, etc., magic, *Once upon a time . . . They all lived happily ever after*, good versus evil, suspense, frightening bits, a happy ending.

3 Tell the class that you are now going to play them four pieces of music, one for each story type. The music tells the beginning of a story or episode. Ask them to listen to the music and write a paragraph telling the story they hear suggested by the music. Play the music. After each piece allow time for them to continue writing. Repeat any of the pieces they ask to hear again.

4 Ask them to choose one of their opening paragraphs and write the rest of the story. This can either be done in class or for homework.

SUGGESTED MUSIC

Detective stories
1 Verdi: *Un ballo in maschera* (*A Masked Ball*), opening of Act I, Scene 2
2 Mahler: Symphony No 1, opening of the fourth movement
3 R. Strauss: *Elektra*, Clytemnestra's murder

Science fiction
1 Wagner: *Das Rheingold,* 'Descent to Nibelheim'
2 Holst: 'Mars' from *The Planets,* opening

Love stories
1 Wagner: Prelude to *Tristan und Isolde*, opening
2 Tchaikovsky: *Romeo and Juliet*, opening

Fairy stories
1 Rimsky-Korsakov: Quintet in B flat, opening of the third movement
2 Mendelssohn: Scherzo from *A Midsummer Night's Dream*, opening

WHAT ELSE HAPPENED?

This exercise combines music and group dynamics to kindle the creativity of the participants. The results are often highly personal and revealing.

Preparation

Choose a piece of music as suggested below.

Procedure

1 A warming-up activity is crucial, something like Activity 1.2 *Follow the Spiral*, Variation 3. Ask your students to keep their eyes closed.
2 Tell your students you are going to play a piece of music that will suggest scenes and events. Add that they should give free rein to their imagination.

4.2

LEVEL
Elementary +

TIME
50 minutes in one lesson; 10–15 in the following lesson

FOCUS
Freer writing; Reading

EXTRAS
Blu-tack or sellotape

3 Play the music and, barely above a whisper, ask: 'What colour can you see? Why? Where is it? What comes to your mind?'

4 When the music has stopped, ask your students to picture the classroom in their minds and slowly open their eyes.

5 Ask your students to write down their impressions in story form. Allow ten minutes for this. Give any help they ask for. Insist that they leave one-third of each page blank (top or bottom).

6 If the class is small and if the classroom is large enough to allow people to move about, everyone puts their sheets up around the room, using Blu-tack or sellotape. The other students walk round the room, read the texts and write questions on the sheets. Whoever writes a question must add their name or initials after it. Walk round and observe. When there are enough questions on the sheets, ask everyone to stop. It is not unusual to have ten questions per story, but take the size of your class and the length of the texts into account.

7 The students get their own sheet back with the questions of the other members of the group. Allow ten minutes for everyone to write the answers to the questions.

8 Everyone takes their sheets home and rewrites their story, incorporating the answers to their classmates' questions.

9 During the next lesson ask your students to hand out their sheets to those who had asked questions, or to fix the sheets on the wall again for rereading and discussion. Finally you can collect the stories for correction of language if you wish.

VARIATION

In large classes – especially if it is difficult to move about in the classroom – put your students into groups of four to six. Ask them to exchange their sheets within the group, to read the texts of the others and to write their questions on their partners' sheets. Then, proceed as in the main activity.

SUGGESTED MUSIC

The excerpt chosen should not be too long (one to two minutes). Too many themes in the music may confuse. Excerpts from the following have worked well in our classes.

1 Berlioz: *Harold in Italy*, Op. 16, (*Harold en Italie*)
  In particular:
  a) first movement ('Harold aux montagnes')
  b) second movement ('Pélerins chantant la prière du soir')
2 Liszt: *Mazeppa*, especially the orchestral version
3 Walton: 'Passacaglia: Death of Falstaff' from 'Henry V Suite'
4 Saint-Saëns: *Phaëton*, the central pursuit theme
5 Saint-Saëns: *Le Rouet d'Omphale*, Finale (Enslavement of Hercules, and Submission)
6 Vaughan Williams: *Sinfonia Antartica*, fifth movement. Choose one of the more suggestive passages with drums, wind, choir, organ, and trumpets.

Here is an (uncorrected) example to give you an idea of the results at mid and end stages. The music used was 'Harold aux montagnes' from *Harold in Italy* by Berlioz.

First version

First I saw red because two people were making love in the dark: the red colour symbolises their passion.

Then I saw green because the woman was walking in nature with a young baby in her arms.

Second version

Jennifer MacDonald is a 24-year old girl of average height. She is nice and very sensitive. She has got hazel brown eyes and curly fair hair.

She is stubborn and she always wants to be right, but she likes joking very much.

Besides she has a special fondness for children: she teaches young pupils.

David Peterson is a handsome boy of 28 with green eyes and straight black hair. He is tall, self-restrained, unsure of himself. He is very kind with his fiancée and always wants to please her.

David and Jennifer have been engaged for two years. They intend to get married soon.

Jennifer would like to have a child, but David has told her that it is impossible so long as he is out of work. As a matter of fact he has been unemployed for 8 months. On a starlit night at the end of summer, Jennifer was lying down on her bed and reading a magazine as she was waiting for her fiancé who had gone off to apply for a job. She was going to sleep when David rushed into the bedroom and told her he had found a job as a mechanic.

They were both so happy that they made love all night long: this was the most beautiful night of their life.

A year later Jennifer could be seen walking in the garden with a baby in her arms.

Two years later she got married to David and they had two other children.

(Annick, girl, 18)

4.3

LEVEL
Upper
intermediate +

TIME
60–90 minutes

FOCUS
Listening for gist
and detail; Raising
awareness of style
in children's
stories

EXTRAS
Multiple copies of
tasksheet (see
Fig. 5)

PETER AND THE WOLF (1) (for higher-level students)

This activity provides an exploitation of Prokofiev's *Peter and the Wolf*, suited to higher-level students. Some of the tasks below (those related to vocabulary) are better suited to upper-intermediate learners, while others (related to style) are aimed at more advanced learners.

In this activity we also explore the effect of the music and its didactic intention, namely to familiarise the listener with the sound of different instruments.

Preparation

1 Decide which of the following tasks are appropriate to the level of your class and what you want to achieve.

2 If you want to do the vocabulary task in Step 5, make a class set of the tasksheet in Fig. 5.

Tasksheet for *Peter and the Wolf 1*

Task 1

The words in the left-hand column are verbs which occur in the story (they are in the correct order). In the right-hand column are synonyms and paraphrases. As you listen to the story, decide which definition goes with which verb.

1	settle	a	happen
2	shrug	b	take, seize
3	crawl	c	bite violently with a noise
4	grab	d	take food or drink from the mouth to the stomach via the
5	perch		throat
6	swallow	e	move the shoulders up and down
7	go on	f	put rope/string round, fix with rope/string
8	stretch out	g	sit on the edge of something
9	snap	h	come to rest
10	tie	i	extend
		j	move along the ground (like a baby that can't walk yet)

Task 2

At the end of the story there is a procession. In what order do the characters come in the procession? Where are the bird and the duck?

Fig. 5   © Longman Group UK Ltd. 1992

Procedure

1 (Optional at upper-intermediate level) Ask your students to think for a moment about children's stories they know. Put them into pairs and ask each pair to make a list of the content and stylistic features of children's stories. Allow about ten minutes and then join the pairs to make groups of four. Tell them to compare their lists. Allow another five minutes for this. Bring the class together again and ask round the class for the various features they wrote down. Write these on the board. Your list might look something like this:

They start with 'Once upon a time . . . '
They end with ' . . . and they all lived happily ever after'
Important child characters – adults less important
Often animal characters – they can talk
Giants, goblins, dwarfs, fairies, genies
Strong differentiation of good and evil
Suspense
Often frightening bits, but happy ending
Fantasy and magic – animals changing to humans, etc.
Things happen that couldn't happen in real life
Simple plot
Vocabulary wide but tendency to use Anglo-Saxon, rather than Latinate
words

2 Tell your students they are going to listen to a story with the
following characters:

a cat
a wolf
a duck
a bird
a boy
his grandfather
hunters

Put your students into groups of three or four. Ask the groups to
guess what happens in the story. Allow up to ten minutes, then ask a
student in each group to tell its story to the rest of the class.

3 Tell your class that the story they are now going to work on is called
Peter and the Wolf and that it is a story told with music. Each
character is represented by a different instrument of the orchestra.
These are the instruments – which one goes with which character?

flute
oboe
clarinet
bassoon
horns
stringed instruments (violins, etc.)
kettle drums and bass drum

When they have decided as far as possible (there may be some where
they feel unable to decide), play the introduction to *Peter and the
Wolf*. This not only gives the answers but plays the theme associated
with each character. The matching is:

flute – bird
oboe – duck
clarinet – cat
bassoon – grandfather
horns – wolf
stringed instruments – Peter
drums – hunters, shooting

4 (With very advanced students, omit this step or do it very quickly.) Check your students know these words, or teach them:

i Ask your class what sounds birds make (include *chirp*).

ii Ask where you would find ducks (include *pond*).

iii Ask how ducks move on water/land (*swim/dive/waddle*) and what kind of sound they make (*quack*).

iv Ask how cats move (*stealthily*) and what cats' feet are called (*paws*).

v Write the word *lasso* on the board. Elicit what it is – a *rope* with a *noose*. Give or mime the example of trying to catch cattle in cowboy films.

5 a Give a copy of the handout to each of your students and give them time to read it. Put them into pairs and tell them to do the tasks as they listen to the story. Ask them also to decide what the music contributes to the story.

b Alternatively, say you are now going to play them the story. Tell them to note any features of children's stories that occur in it. Ask them also to decide what the music contributes to the story.

6 Play the story.

7 a If you did Step 5a, tell the pairs of students to check they agree about the answers on the handout. Go over them together.

For Task 1 the words and definitions match as follows:

1h, 2e, 3j, 4b, 5g, 6d, 7a, 8i, 9c, 10f.

For Task 2 the order in the procession is:

Peter; the hunters; the wolf; grandfather and the cat.

The bird was flying around overhead; the duck was still alive in the wolf's stomach.

Task 2 is very simple but it provides the students with a focus for the latter part of the story.

b If you did Step 5b, check with the class which features they found. There are good examples of most things.

8 Ask the class how they felt the music contributed to the story. Most people find that it provides both psychic space and stimulation to allow the imagination full rein. This helps the listener to visualise much better what is going on in the story. Ask your students, by way of example, how many hunters there were and what their age was. They usually agree that there were about half a dozen fairly elderly hunters, but this is purely the result of visualisation from the music and is not mentioned in the text.

9 Tell your class that Prokofiev's objective in writing *Peter and the Wolf* was to help children to recognise musical instruments from their sound. Ask them how successful they think the attempt was. What did they learn from the experience?

EXTENSION

Ask the students to write a children's story.

ACKNOWLEDGEMENT

We owe the ideas on style and children's stories to Jennifer Nunes.

PETER AND THE WOLF 2
(for lower-level students)

Prokofiev wrote *Peter and the Wolf* for children, to help them recognise the instruments of the orchestra. This activity, which works well with adults too, exploits the potential of the piece for generating communicative use of a foreign language. (We would advise you not to do this activity with youngsters at the 'silly age' of 13–15.)

Preparation

Before each lesson make a class set of copies of the pictures to be used (see Fig. 6).

Procedure

LESSON 1

1 Tell your students they are going to hear a story with the following characters:

a cat	a boy
a wolf	his grandfather
a duck	hunters
a bird	

Put your students into groups of three or four. Ask the groups to guess what they think happened in the story. Allow up to ten minutes, then ask a student in each group to tell its story to the rest of the class.

2 Tell your class that the story they are going to work on is called *Peter and the Wolf* and that it is a story told with music. Give each student a set of these character pictures.

Fig. 6

4.4

LEVEL
Children aged 10–12 or adults; Good elementary to intermediate

TIME
Do this over a series of three lessons.
Lesson 1: 40–50 minutes
Lesson 2: 20 minutes
Lesson 3: 40–60 minutes

FOCUS
Listening for gist, oral story-telling

EXTRAS
For each lesson: multiple copies of the story pictures (see Figs. 6–9).
For lesson 1: pictures of musical instruments (if possible)
For Extension 1: plain white paper and paints/crayons; large pieces of card and glue (optional); blu-tack, sellotape or drawing pins

Fig. 6 cont.

3 Tell them that in the story each character is represented by a different instrument of the orchestra. The instruments are:

flute
oboe
clarinet
bassoon
horns
stringed instruments (violins, etc.)
kettle drums and bass drum

4 If possible, show them labelled photos of the instruments. Tell them you are going to play the introduction to *Peter and the Wolf*. Ask them to listen and write the name of the instrument that goes with each character on the correct picture. Play the introduction. This not only gives the answers but plays the theme for each character.

5 Go through the answers with them. The matching is:

flute – bird
oboe – duck
clarinet – cat
bassoon – grandfather
horns – wolf
stringed instruments – Peter
drums – hunters, shooting

6 Check your students know these essential words, otherwise teach them: *gate, branch, pond*.

7 Tell your class that they are going to hear the first part of the story today and the rest over the next two lessons. Give out copies of the pictures for Part 1 (see Fig. 7 overleaf). Tell them that the pictures tell the first part of the story but in the wrong order. Ask them to write a number from 1 to 6 beside each picture to indicate the order in the story as they hear it.

8 Play the story as far as when grandfather comes out and says, 'If a wolf should come out of the forest, then what would you do?' Ask your students which is the first picture in the story. Then the second, and so on. The correct order is:

1 – top right
2 – bottom right
3 – top left
4 – centre left
5 – centre right
6 – bottom left

9 Ask your students what they think will happen next in the story. They are almost certain to say that a wolf does come out of the forest. So ask them to work with a partner and try to predict what will happen after that. Tell them to write down their prediction, so they can refer back to it next lesson. When they are ready, ask round the room to see what predictions they have made.

Fig. 7

LESSON 2

1 Tell your class they are going to hear the second part of *Peter and the Wolf*. Ask them what has happened so far in the story. Refer them to their predictions from the end of last lesson. What do they expect to happen next?

2 Give out copies of the pictures in Fig. 8 and tell them to write a number from 7 to 10 beside each picture to indicate the order in the story.

Fig. 8

3 Play the story as far as the words: 'And the wolf walked round and round the tree looking at them with greedy eyes.'

4 Check the answers as before (Lesson 1, Step 8, page 51). The correct order is:

    7 – bottom left
    8 – top left
    9 – bottom right
    10 – top right

5 Again, as before, ask the students with a partner to write a prediction of what will happen next in the story. When they are ready, ask your class to tell you their predictions.

LESSON 3

As well as the multiple copies, assemble the materials for the extension.

1 Tell your class they are going to hear the last part of *Peter and the Wolf*. Ask them what has happened in the second part of the story. Refer them to their predictions from the end of last lesson. What do they expect to happen next? Tell them that the next part of the story will involve a lasso. Explain what a lasso is by miming a cowboy catching a cow. Ask them what they now think will happen in the story.

2 Give out copies of the pictures in Fig. 9 opposite and tell them to write a number from 11 to 15 beside each picture to indicate the order in the story.

3 Play the story as far as when Peter says: 'Now help us to take him to the zoo.'

4 Check the answers as before (Lesson 1, Step 8 and Lesson 2, Step 4). The correct order is:

    11 – top right
    12 – bottom
    13 – top left
    14 – centre right
    15 – centre left

5 Tell your class that in a few moments the characters form a procession. Ask them to write down what order the characters come in and where the bird and the duck are.

6 Play the rest of the story.

7 Ask them about the order in the procession. The correct order is:

    Peter; the hunters; the wolf; grandfather and the cat.

Ask about the bird and the duck. The bird was flying overhead and the duck was still alive in the wolf's stomach.

Fig. 9

EXTENSION 1

1 (For children) Tell your students you would like them to make a picture of the procession. Give them paper and crayons or paints. They can either do their pictures individually or divide into groups of seven, each doing one character and then mounting them on a large piece of card. If you go for the second option, set up the groups, get them to decide who does what, monitor the cooperation carefully and provide the card and glue when they are all ready.

2 As the pictures are completed, help your students to mount them on the classroom wall with Blu-tack, sellotape or drawing pins so that everyone can see.

EXTENSION 2

(For children or adults) Tell your students to write a story using the same characters but ending: 'The wolf and the duck lived happily ever after.'

EXTENSION 3

1 (For children or adults) Tell your students you would like to dramatise the story of *Peter and the Wolf*. You would like them to write the script and eventually act it out.

2 Divide your class into groups of seven – the number of characters. (Any students left over can become additional hunters.) Tell the groups to decide who is going to play which part and then to write the script. The person playing each part must contribute the words he or she is going to say in the 'play'. Be available to help as needed while they are writing the script. When it is ready, help them to correct it. Ask them to memorise their lines for next lesson.

3 Next lesson have the different groups act out their version to the rest of the class. Ask them as they watch to decide which they think is the best version and why. After you have seen all of the 'plays' discuss this with your class. Award a prize for the best version – you may have to offer several if they don't agree!

ACKNOWLEDGEMENT

We owe the idea of a drama extension to Jennifer Nunes.

INSTANT DRAMA

A sceptical student's initial reaction:

I am really puzzled by people's ability to see things in music. I can't. Take this music for example . . . if you ask me, I would visualise a train steaming through the prairie and Indians attacking it . . . while some people are desperately trying to defend it . . .

The music was Honegger's *Pacific 231*, which purports to describe a train, the Pacific 231, driving full speed through America.

NOTE
If your group is not too large everyone can take an active role. Otherwise those who cannot take part actively, act as furniture and props, or are spectators.

Preparation

Choose a piece of music that creates a certain atmosphere. 'Dramatic' music will generate a dramatic story, serene music is likely to evoke a fairy tale. Some music is suggested below. In the Procedure we take as an example a section from Honegger's *Pacific 231*.

Procedure

1 Explain that there is a kind of drama called a 'happening', where the actors invent the plot on the spur of the moment and then act it out together with the public. Tell your students they are going to have an opportunity to create a play like that. First they are going to hear some music that will be the starting point for their plot. They themselves are going to decide what takes place, and they will then play the drama in class.
2 Get your students to concentrate. (Any of the Variations of Activity 1.1 *Focusing* would be suitable.) Next, play the music. Your students jot down words about the ideas that the music generates.
3 At plot development stage, your role as a teacher is crucial, but should be as discreet as possible. Here are some ways in which you can enable the plot to develop in the whole-class session.
   i To leave as much room as possible to your students' imagination try to limit your interventions to monosyllabic questions such as: 'Who?', 'Where?' 'Why?', 'How?', 'When?'
   ii If necessary, get your students started by asking a longer question. For example: 'Is it something that happened in a town, in the country, on a mountain?' Whatever the group accepts as valid by consensus is adopted.
   iii As the plot takes shape, encourage the class to elaborate by asking more specific questions such as: 'What kind of train?' 'What time of day?', 'What season?', 'What carriage?', 'Describe the carriage', 'Is there someone in the carriage?', 'Describe the person'.

4.5

LEVEL
Intermediate +

TIME
50 minutes or more

FOCUS
Oral expression; Non-verbal expression

EXTRAS
None

REQUIREMENT
A classroom affording room to move about in the centre

    iv When one episode has been created, encourage the class to go on by asking 'And then?', 'And after that?' or simply 'And?' or even 'Mmm?' or putting on a questioning look. Keep up a brisk pace. Once the flow of ideas has started, proposals should gush from everywhere.

4 The class gradually builds up the story: the setting becomes clear, the characters come to life, and the plot develops with the members of the class as authors. Provide any vocabulary they need. Correct inconsistencies by repeating the story line now and then, or by asking a student to do this. This is a useful listening comprehension exercise and provides the help needed by weaker students.

5 Keep things moving briskly. If things begin to drag after a few episodes, provide a quick ending yourself.

6 Agree on roles for acting out. Since as many students as possible should take part in the performance, some participants can be objects, while others can provide sound effects. Allow your students to choose which part they play. Take on an embarrassing role yourself if necessary. Accept all gestures and mimicry that do not create problems for others or yourself.

EXTENSION

Ask your students to write the end, or the sequel at home.

RATIONALE

Body language and verbal language are used in a way which can be deeply relevant to the learners. Even if the story is 'silly' as seen from the outside, something of the collective subconscious of the group will emerge. Language used and learned in this way will really stay in their minds.

SUGGESTED MUSIC

Choose a piece of about three minutes.

1 Holst: The Finale of 'Mars' from *The Planets* (very unpredictable results, but invariably dramatic)

2 Copland: *Billy the Kid* (particularly suitable for younger learners)

3 Arne: Sonata No. 1 in F, for Harpsichord. Take the Andante to generate a fairy-tale-like play.

4 Gershwin: Piano Concerto in F, third movement

5 Beethoven: Symphony No. 3 ('Eroica'), first movement

6 Honegger: *Pacific 231* (Mouvement Symphonique No. 1). Take a three-minute selection just before the end. This often yields a play in the style of *Murder on the Orient Express*, or a scene on the American prairie with cowboys and Indians attacking a train.

ACKNOWLEDGEMENT

The idea to use music to create 'instant drama' took shape during exercises with bankers at the Royal Bank of Canada.

CHAPTER 5

Music and people

'Music is as characteristically human as language.'

In this chapter we link music and people. In Activity 5.1 *Musical characters* and Activity 5.7 *Friends* your students listen to music in which the composer was consciously trying to describe someone. In the other activities the connection between the music and the people is less clearly defined. They are more concerned with links that you and your students make between music and people, including yourselves. In general the activities in this chapter have a particularly positive effect on the dynamic of the class.

MUSICAL CHARACTERS

You can do this activity several times, using different music and introducing new words every time.

Preparation

Choose a piece of music as suggested below.

Procedure

1 Explain to your students that some musical compositions are intended to portray people, and add that they are going to try to describe the person they hear in a short piece of music. Ask them to take notes while they listen.
2 Play the music you have chosen (twice if the students ask you to). Give your students some time afterwards to look up any words they need in the *Longman Lexicon* or a good bilingual dictionary. They can also ask their classmates and yourself for help.
3 In groups of four, students try to find points in common in their descriptions. The group appoints a student to report to the class.
4 When possible, give the students a description of the person the composer had in mind. You can read out a description in a few sentences, or hand out a text written by the composer or by the author who gave the original idea to the composer.
5 The learners discuss in groups in what ways their perception is similar or different to the composer's.
6 Alternatively, allow the class to ask you twenty *Yes/No* questions to find out how close they are to the composer's idea.

5.1

LEVEL
Elementary +

TIME
20 minutes +
(according to the level)

FOCUS
Describing people;
Discussion

EXTRAS
A text about the character described by the music (for intermediate + students)

EXTENSION

Invite your students to bring music to class (or to come and play music) that they feel describes themselves. The class discusses how far they feel the music describes the student.

VARIATION

(for Richard Strauss's *Till Eulenspiegel*)

1 Put your students in groups of three or four. Ask what kind of person they think is described by the music. Invite them to imagine this person physically, where he or she lived and what kind of things she or he did. Play a two-minute excerpt from the beginning.

2 Allow the students to talk it over in groups, and a secretary reports to the class.

3 Tell your students Till Eulenspiegel (Till Owlglass) was a prankster, and hand out the list of pranks below.

> 1 Till's father rides through town with his son behind him on his horse. Till shows everyone his bottom, and the people shout at him.
>
> 2 Till rides to the marketplace on his donkey which tramples the market women's pottery to bits. They shout at him but Till rides off, making faces.
>
> 3 Till works for a miserly baker who wants him to sift the flour in the moonlight, which Till does literally. He sifts the flour on the ground where the moon shines. The baker is very angry.
>
> 4 Till, disguised as a priest, says a sermon. When his listeners realise they have been made fun of, Till has already scarpered.
>
> 5 Till sees a pretty girl and falls in love, which is against his deeper nature. She refuses him.
>
> 6 Till meets three blind men and pretends to give them three shillings. They go to an inn to have a meal. When the time has come to pay, nobody has the money. They accuse each other of keeping the money for themselves. The innkeeper is very angry and throws them out.
>
> 7 Till pretends to be a great scholar and makes fun of university dons who challenge him.

4 Tell your students only some of the pranks are described musically, and ask them to listen once more and to decide which ones they can hear. Play the rest of the music (about twelve minutes). (The pranks that Strauss had in mind are 2, 4, 5 and 7, in that order. The others are not depicted in the music.) Finally, Till is sentenced to death, but his conclusion is 'Even gods fight stupidity in vain'.)

5 Tell the class which ones are actually described in the music. Allow students who got some right to explain what associations they made between the music and the pranks.

6 Ask your students to write a composition for a later lesson. Possible titles, e.g.:
- 'A trick I played on someone'
- 'A joke I enjoyed'
- 'A prank I did not find funny'.

7 Photocopy a class set of the compositions so that all the students read each other's compositions at home, and in a later lesson they can vote to decide which one is the funniest. The winner gets an Eulenspiegel award. (Decide with the class what it should be.)

SUGGESTED MUSIC

1 Saint-Saëns: 'The lion' from *Carnival of the Animals*, (1 min 30) Students usually describe a strong, tall, arrogant person.

2 Mussorgsky (orchestrated by Ravel): *Pictures at an Exhibition*
   a) 'Gnomus' (2 min 30) This piece should suggest the eerie shape of a gnome and his waddling, awkward physical movements.
   b) 'Samuel Goldenberg and Schmuyle' (2 min 30) Interesting to use when the students have got used to this kind of exercise, as there is a dialogue between two people here; one rich and laconic, the other poor and restless.

3 Holst: 'Saturn, the Bringer of Old Age' from *The Planets*, the two minutes at the beginning. This suggests the calm, serenity and slow pace of old people.

4 Richard Strauss: *Till Eulenspiegel*. In this piece Strauss describes a mischievous character, Till Eulenspiegel, who plays pranks on everyone. Works with the main activity and the variation.

5 Nielsen: Symphony No. 2, 'The Four Temperaments'. Each of the movements describes a different kind of person in a very expressionistic way. This is ideal to practise describing people several times. Here are some texts from Nielsen himself, in which he describes what kind of people he had in mind. Select a three-minute excerpt from the movement you have chosen.
   a) First movement: Allegro collerico
   Nielsen recollected the picture on which he based his music as portraying a man on horseback with a long sword in his hand:

   His eyes were nearly rolling out of his head, his hair flew madly round his face; it was so full of fury and devilish hate that I burst into laughter.

   b) Second movement: Allegro comodo e flemmatico
   Nielsen tells us that he visualised a youngster of about seventeen or eighteen, the despair of his teachers who gave up on him because he never knew his lessons:

   But it was impossible to scold him, for everything idyllic and heavenly was to be found in this young lad, so that every one was disarmed. His real inclination was to lie where the birds sing, where the fish glide noiselessly through the water, where the sun warms and the wind strokes mildly round one's curls. He was fair; his expression was rather happy, but not self-complacent, rather with a hint of quiet melancholy, so that one felt impelled to be good to him. When the air was shimmering in the heat, he would usually be lying on the pier at the harbour, with his legs dangling over the edge. I have never seen him dance; he wasn't active enough for that, though he might easily have got the idea to swing himself in a gentle slow waltz rhythm.

c) Third movement: Andante malincolico

I have tried to express the basic character of a heavy melancholy man.

d) Fourth movement: Allegro sanguineo

In the finale I have tried to sketch a man who storms thoughtlessly forward in the belief that the whole world belongs to him, that fried pigeons will fly into his mouth without worry or bother. There is though a moment in which something scares him, and he gasps all at once for breath in rough syncopations: but this is soon forgotten and . . . his cheery superficial nature still asserts itself.

As quoted by Robert Layton: *Nielsen's Symphonies and Concertos,* notes for the EMI recording of Nielsen's symphonies and concertos (1975)

6 R. Strauss: *Don Juan,* opening 2–3 minutes

7 Debussy: *Général Lavine,* from Préludes, Book I (2 min 45).

5.2

LEVEL
Intermediate +

TIME
15–20 minutes

FOCUS
Oral or written expression; Describing people

EXTRAS
Three or four portraits of very different people

MUSICAL PORTRAITS
Preparation

1 Find three or four portraits of very different people. If the pictures are not large enough for everyone in the class to see easily, you need a class set. Reproductions of painted portraits, or photographs are ideal, but you can use magazine pictures as well. Slides are perfect. Here is an example of a set of portraits we have used in class.

Fig. 10a

Fig. 10b

Fig. 10c

Fig. 10d

The following painted portraits would be very suitable since in these examples there are several kinds of contrasts. Not only are the people different, but the styles of the portraits are distinctive too.

Set 1

1 John Getty: *Portrait of John Harper* (York City Art Gallery)
2 Dante Gabriel Rossetti: *Joli Coeur* (Manchester City Art Galleries)
3 Pieter Brueghel: *The Yawner* (Royal Museum of Ancient Arts, Brussels)

Set 2

1 Dante Gabriel Rossetti: *Beata Beatrix* (Tate Gallery, London, 1863)
2 R. Van der Weyden: *Philip de Croy* (Royal Museum of Fine Arts, Antwerp)
3 Augustus John: *Matthew Smith* (Tate Gallery London, TG NO5929)

Set 3

1 Stanley Spencer: *Self-portrait* (Tate Gallery, London, TG NO6188)
2 Pablo Picasso: *Seated Woman in a Chemise* (Tate Gallery, London, TG NO4719)
3 John Opie: *Master William Opie* (Tate Gallery, London, TG NO1408)

2 Choose a piece of music that you feel can be linked with one of the people in the portraits. There may be a connection with any of the following: the style of the portrait, the person's temperament, age, expression, clothes, profession, etc.

Procedure

1 Hand out, display or project the portraits.
2 Ask your students to write down what distinguishes the three portraits from each other (physique, age, clothes, expression, position in society . . .) The *Longman Lexicon* would be very helpful here.
3 Play the music.
4 Ask your students to decide which portrait fits the music and to jot down a few words (not sentences) to explain their choice.
5 In pairs the students explain the reasons for making their choice, but without saying what that choice is. Each partner tries to discover what the other has chosen. Finally they discuss their choices.

VARIATION

Alternatively, bring in one portrait and choose three very different pieces of music. Your students try to associate one of the pieces with the portrait.
For example:
Take a portrait of a dignified old man and play:
a) A nocturne by Field or Chopin
b) A spirited violin tune, such as Paganini's 'Moto perpetuo'
c) An excerpt from a violin sonata by Ysaÿe.

Encourage your students to bring portraits of people they know and also music to associate with them. In a later lesson they can direct an activity. The student leaders can round off the activity by stating their reasons for linking a portrait with a particular piece of music.

5.3

LEVEL
Intermediate +

TIME
15 minutes

FOCUS
Speaking about moods and states of mind; Getting students to know each other better

EXTRAS
An OHP transparency with words describing moods (optional)

MUSICAL MOODS

Preparation

1 Decide what kind of moods you would like your students to speak about. If you wish, prepare a transparency with the vocabulary needed.
Here are some examples of moods you can deal with:
- joy, happiness, excitement, elation, exhilaration, triumph
- serenity, peacefulness, calm, tranquillity, self-possession
- pain, sorrow, grief, sadness, despair, bereavement, misery
- regret, melancholy, longing, wistfulness, nostalgia, yearning
- fear, alarm, anxiety, apprehension, terror, foreboding.
2 Choose three short excerpts (one to two minutes each) appropriate for the moods you have chosen to deal with.

Procedure

1 Explain to your students that hardly any musician escapes expressing their mood in the music they compose or interpret.
2 Ask everyone to listen carefully to the three excerpts you have prepared and to write down the mood they feel the composer is expressing in the music.
3 Ask them to think of moments in their lives when they were in the mood they hear in the music, and to write this down in note form. While they do this, help other students to find the exact English word that expresses the mood they have in mind.
4 Your students choose a partner and exchange their impressions about the mood they have attributed to the music, speaking about the circumstances when they were in such a mood.
5 Elicit from the class the different moods they have perceived in the music. Write these on the board. Help the students to find near-synonyms that express the moods more precisely still.
6 To enable the students to exchange their impressions with another student and to develop their vocabulary, ask them to choose another partner to talk about their mood again, starting from the new words they have just studied.

EXTENSION 1
Encourage your students to bring in music that they feel reflects one of their moods. The class can either try to describe the mood, or ask twenty *Yes/No* questions.

EXTENSION 2

Invite students to read out loud a text (a poem, a haiku or a prose text) that they feel describes one of their moods. It can be a text written by the student or it can be a literary text. Ask the class to find music that would fit this mood. Students who feel they can propose a musical equivalent bring it in a later lesson. They play the music and discuss it in class. This brings out very warm feelings when the student agrees with the choice of another student. This works even better if students can actually play the music themselves.

EXTENSION 3

Composition: 'My musical moods'

If necessary, explain that they can speak about the kind of music they need when they are in certain moods, or about the music that best renders their moods. We often give them free rein and accept any kind of work (poem, poetic prose, essay). Musical illustrations are welcome!

SUGGESTED MUSIC

Joy and happiness

1 Paganini: Concerto for Violin and Orchestra No. 5 in A minor, excerpts from the first movement (Allegro maestoso), especially the violin solos
2 Mozart: Flute Concerto No. 1, K 313, first movement
3 Albinoni: Concerto in D minor for Oboe and Strings, Op. 9 No. 2
4 Handel: 'Arrival of the Queen of Sheba', from *Solomon*
5 Vivaldi: Piccolo Concerto in C, PV 78/RV444, first and last movements
6 Verdi: 'Triumphal March' from *Aida*
7 J.S. Bach: Brandenburg Concerto No. 6, first movement

Serenity and calm

1 Pachelbel: Canon in D
2 Telemann: Quartet in D minor for Recorder, two Flutes and Continuo, an excerpt from any of the movements
3 Alessandro Scarlatti: Concerto in A minor ('Sonata Nona'), for Descant Recorders, two Violins and Basso Continuo, first and second movements
4 Handel: Oboe Concerto No. 3 in G minor
5 Mozart: Andante in C, K 315
6 Japanese shakuhachi music, especially in the Zen-derived classical honkyoku style which usually exudes serenity
7 Vietnamese classical music: 'Không Minh toa lâu' ('Không Minh at the balcony')

Pain and distress

1 Nielsen: *At the Bier of a Young Artist (Ved en ung Kunstners Baare)*
2 Richard Strauss: *Death and Transfiguration (Tod und Verklärung) Op. 14,* excerpts from the beginning
3 Mozart: *Requiem*
4 Bruch: Violin Concerto No. 1 in G minor, Op. 26, opening of the second movement

5 Beethoven: Symphony No. 3 ('Eroica'), parts of the second movement
6 Josquin des Prés: 'Déploration, à la mort de Jean Ockeghem' ('Nymphes des bois')

Regret and nostalgia

1 Vieuxtemps: Violin Concerto No. 5 in A minor, Op. 37, second movement ('Where can one better feel?' – 'Où peut-on être mieux?' – theme after Grétry's *Lucille*)
2 Smetana: *Má vlast: Vyšehrad*
3 Beethoven: 'Für Elise'
4 Butterworth: *A Shropshire Lad*
5 Dvořák: String Quartet in F ('The American'), second movement
6 Wagner: *Tannhäuser*, Overture
7 Vietnamese classical music: 'Song of the monochord' (*Độc Huyên Câm Khúc*)
8 Elgar: Violin Concerto, fourth movement, the rhapsodic, cadenza-like solo over tremulous, pizzicato string chords

Fear and apprehension

1 Wagner: *Tristan and Isolde*, Prelude
2 Stenhammar: Interlude from the cantata 'Sången', Op. 44
3 Brahms: *Tragic Overture*, Op. 81. Choose passages with the ominous roll on the timpani.
4 Rossini: *William Tell*, Act III, the cello solo at 'Sois immobile' (as Tell is about to shoot the apple off his son's head)
5 Verdi: *Un ballo in maschera* (*A Masked Ball*), orchestral opening of Act I, Scene 2
6 Stravinsky: *Rite of Spring (Le Sacre du Printemps)*, beginning of final section 'Danse Sacrale'

5.4

LEVEL
Intermediate +

TIME
15 minutes

FOCUS
Speaking; *Yes/No* questions; Making hypotheses; Getting to know each other better

EXTRAS
None

MUSIC IN MY LIFE

This exercise works best when you and your students still do not know each other too well, a couple of weeks after the beginning of the course for instance.

Preparation

Choose a piece of music lasting a maximum of three minutes that is important for you because it has a link with some event, person or place in your life. In less advanced classes choose a piece where the link is not too difficult to find.

Procedure

1 Tell your students you are going to play a piece of music that has a special meaning for you. Explain that you expect them to find out why by asking twenty questions you can answer with *yes* or *no*.
2 Play the music.

Here are some questions that students have asked:
- Is it some music you play yourself?
- Do you like the instruments?
- Do you associate this music with a place?
- Do you associate this music with some person?
- Was it a woman?
- Did you marry that woman?

etc.

3 If they have not come to a precise solution after twenty questions, ask the students to talk it over in groups of four, and to agree on a tentative explanation. A spokesperson for each group then presents the group version.

4 Say which one is closest to reality.

5 Finally tell them what the music means to you.

EXTENSION

Encourage students to bring in music that is important to them and to come and answer questions about it.

WHO LIKES THIS MUSIC?

Preparation

Choose a short piece of music that someone you know well likes very much.

Procedure

1 Start by telling your students that particular kinds of people like particular kinds of music, and that there is a link between people's character, and even their physique, and the music they like. Before playing the music tell an anecdote that shows how much the person whose music you are going to play likes it.

2 Play the music, twice if your class asks for it. Students write what comes to mind about the person who likes it. Suggest they speak about the person's age, sex, build, character, and things he or she likes or likes doing. Encourage everyone to look up or ask for any words they need.

3 Put your class into groups of four to try to come to a consensus. Appoint a secretary for each group. Move from group to group to monitor what is happening in order to encourage and help with vocabulary.

4 Ask the secretary in each group to present the results of their discussion. If a group hasn't achieved consensus, allow it to present more than one opinion.

5 Ask the class if they would like to know if what they have said corresponds to the facts. If so, confirm anything said that was right.

6 Elicit more questions to bring out additional facts.

5.5

LEVEL
Intermediate +

TIME
15–20 minutes

FOCUS
Describing people (character and physique); Discussion; Asking questions; Linking people and the music they like

EXTRAS
None

VARIATION 1

If possible, have the music actually played by the person who likes it. This will heighten interest, as the way the music is played will also give clues about the person. It need not be a highly professional perform- ance, on the contrary, the spontaneity of an amateur rendering often loosens up the class.

VARIATION 2

1 After Step 3, hand out a copy of a text in which you describe the person, but where a number of facts are not true. Ask your students to look for elements in the text that correspond to their guesses and that they believe to be true.

2 Appoint a spokesperson to report in what ways the description agreed on by their group is similar to the text and why.

3 Round off the exercise by saying what elements were incorrect.

VARIATION 3

After playing the music, play a recorded text in which the 'subject' explains why he or she likes the music. Then go on as described in Steps 2–6.

5.6

MUSICAL BATH

LEVEL
Intermediate +

TIME
15 minutes

FOCUS
Talking about temperatures; Expressing opinions (agreeing, disagreeing, identifying, giving reasons); Matching people and their musical tastes; Exchanging ideas about musical tastes; Helping students to know each other better

EXTRAS
Optional: an OHP and transparency

Do this activity when the students know each other up to a point, but not too well yet. You need to have found out what kinds of music they like before you do this exercise.

Preparation

Choose five musical excerpts of about thirty seconds each. Your choice should be made in the light of what you know your students as a whole like and do not like in music. Try to represent most tastes. Include different musical genres and definitely some songs.

If possible, prepare an OHP transparency with the drawing of a thermometer with five graduations: *Far too hot, Too hot, Just right, Too cold, Brr . . . freezing*.

Procedure

1 If you have the transparency, project it, otherwise draw a thermo- meter with the five graduations on the board. Ask your students to copy it.

2 Say that the first thing people usually express about music is whether they like it or not. This is also true of a bath or a shower. They are going to match their reaction to music and how they feel about the temperature of the water when they have a bath or shower.

3 Tell them they are going to listen to five short musical excerpts. You want them to write the number of each one beside the thermometer

mark describing their reaction to that piece of music. If they can, they should try to identify the excerpts. It is essential that their neighbours do not see what they are writing. Play the excerpts.

4 Play them all a second time to allow your students to rethink their ordering as their standards may have changed as they listened to the remaining pieces.

5 Form pairs that do not know each other too well, though not complete strangers either. Tell everyone to try to guess how their partner has reacted to the different excerpts. Student A guesses, and Student B puts A right in the case of a wrong guess. Then B says more, e.g.: 'First I liked it because I liked the voice, but I didn't like the tune . . .'; 'I used to like this when I was younger, but I have changed.' They can then count how many of the guesses were right. Then swap. Also, they should try to agree on the identification of the excerpts, being as detailed as they can: 'This must be a nineteenth-century piano nocturne.' Or just: 'It is a guitar solo, I suspect it is Spanish music . . .'

6 Ask if anyone guessed their partner's choice perfectly (five out of five), who got four out of five etc.

7 Invite the class as a whole to try and identify the excerpts one by one. Praise your students whenever they've got part of the identification right.

FRIENDS

Fig. 11

5.7

LEVEL
Intermediate +

TIME
20–40 minutes

FOCUS
Talking about people

EXTRAS
The photograph reproduced in Fig. 11

In this activity we provide an opportunity to talk about people we are fond of – family and friends – and build this round Elgar's *Enigma Variations*.

Preparation

Select three of the *Enigma Variations* to play in Step 4. A particularly good group for our purposes are Variations 7, 8 and 9 (Troyte, W.N. and Nimrod).

Procedure

1 Ask your students to write down the names of three friends or relatives they are especially fond of. Then tell them to write a few words beside each name explaining why they appreciate these friends. Here are two examples for David:

Robin   – my brother
           – though he lives a long way away, he's always there
           – he's a very kind, generous person
           – he's very astute, so I can put some of my mad ideas to him and see how he reacts

Manzoor – my best friend
           – he's very patient and sympathetic with me (not always easy!)
           – though I don't often see him, I always feel it's as if we'd never been apart
           – he helped me through a difficult patch some years ago

Divide the class into groups of three or four and ask the students to tell the others in their group about the people they've written about.

2 Show your students the photograph reproduced in Fig. 11. Don't tell them anything about it and if there is anyone in the class you think might recognise the man, ask them not to tell anyone else at this stage. Ask the class in their groups to speculate as to what kind of man they think this is (e.g. profession, character, single or married, with children?) and what kind of friends they think he might have (e.g. older/younger, male/female, character, class). Ask one person in each group to act as secretary and write down the group's thoughts. Allow five minutes for this.

3 Bring the class back together and ask each group secretary in turn to report what their group thought. Then tell your students (or if one of the students recognises the photo, ask them to do so) that it is a picture of Edward Elgar (1857–1934), the English composer, and that among the pieces he wrote were the *Enigma Variations* (1899), which were a series of character sketches of his friends and himself. Tell them they are going to listen to three of these.

4 Tell your students as they listen to decide for themselves (without consulting colleagues) whether they think that each of these friends is male/female, older/younger/about the same age as the composer (he was forty-one when he composed the music) and what kind of character they had. Play the music.

5 Put the students back into their groups. Ask them to compare what they thought, appoint a secretary (a different one from last time) to

report the group's ideas to the rest of the class. Allow about five minutes for this. Chair feedback from the group secretaries.

We have found a certain amount of agreement as regards the character the students hear, but the sex is often far from clear. People tend to disagree about Troyte; W.N. is usually heard as female; Nimrod is more often male, but inevitably heard as someone very close to the composer (best friend, wife, self). For information on the characters portrayed in the *Enigma Variations*, see Note 1.

NOTES

1 The composer indicated in the score who was being portrayed in each variation. These indications are given below with a brief explanation.

Theme

Variation 1 C.A.E. (Alice Elgar, the composer's wife)

Variation 2 H.D.S.-P. (Hew David Steuart-Powell, a pianist friend with whom he played chamber music)

Variation 3 R.B.T. (Richard Baxter Townshend, a friend with a funny voice and manner)

Variation 4 W.M.B. (William Meath Baker a country squire, gentleman and scholar)

Variation 5 R.P.A. (Richard P. Arnold, an amateur pianist and something of a wit)

Variation 6 Ysobel (Isabel Fitton, a viola-player and member of a music-loving family the Elgars knew well)

Variation 7 Troyte (Arthur Troyte Griffith, an architect from Malvern and a lifelong close friend)

Variation 8 W.N. (Winifred Norbury, a music-loving friend)

Variation 9 Nimrod (August Johannes Jaeger, who worked for his publisher, Novello, and was both critic and close friend)

Variation 10 Dorabella (Dora Penny, musical and merry, a frequent guest of the Elgars)

Variation 11 G.R.S. (Dr G.R. Sinclair, organist of Hereford Cathedral, and his dog, Dan)

Variation 12 B.G.N. (Basil G. Nevinson, amateur cellist and third member, with Steuart-Powell, of the composer's piano trio)

Variation 13 *** (identity not known for certain)

Variation 14 E.D.U. (the composer; 'Edoo' was what his wife called him)

2 You can obtain postcards of the photograph from the National Portrait Gallery, St Martin's Place, London WC2H 0HE. Ask for the photograph of Sir Edward Elgar by Herbert Lambert, 1933 (ref. P107).

ACKNOWLEDGEMENT

We obtained the information about Elgar's friends from *Portrait of Elgar* (Kennedy 1987).

CHAPTER 6

Nature

'Music is the sound of life.'
(Carl Nielsen)

This chapter reflects the great source of inspiration that nature has always been to musicians. The first three activities link music and landscape. In these we have chosen music which composers wrote to evoke images of landscape and exploited them so that they do precisely that. Thus they provide your students with a stimulus for a 'guided fantasy' and an opportunity to make imaginative use of the language they've been working on to describe landscapes. The same principle applies to Activity 6.4 *Seasons and times of day* and Activity 6.5 *Weather*, but with other aspects of nature. The final activity, 6.6, *The music of nature* involves using sounds taken directly from nature.

6.1

LEVEL
Intermediate +

TIME
30–50 minutes

FOCUS
Writing descriptions of places; Reading (optional)

EXTRAS
None

DESCRIBE THE SCENE

For this activity use Rossini's Overture to *William Tell*. Do it as a follow-up to language input on describing places.

Procedure

1 On the board draw up two columns. At the head of the first write the word *rural* and at the head of the other write *urban*. Elicit different types of rural and urban landscape. Write the types in the columns. Your board might look something like this:

rural	urban
rivers and streams	streets and lanes
meadows	villages
hills and mountains	inner cities
plains	factories and industry
heaths	houses
coast and sea	
woods and forest	

2 Briefly elicit the kinds of things you would find in each place.
3 Tell your students you are going to play them a piece of music in three sections, each of which describes a scene. Ask them, as they listen, to write a description of the scene they hear. Tell them that the piece is quite well known. If they know it, they should not tell anyone else. Play the first three sections of the Rossini overture. After each

section, pause to allow the students to continue writing if they wish. When they are ready, go on to the next section.

4 After they have all finished writing, ask the class what kind of scene they heard, referring to your list on the board. Or was it some kind of scene which no one mentioned in the earlier part of the lesson?

5 If time allows in class, ask your students to refine and correct their descriptions in collaboration with a partner. If you are short of time, ask them to do this for homework.

6 As the students are leaving at the end of the lesson, play the final 'Galop' section of the overture – the part that everyone knows.

NOTE

According to the composer, the music describes Alpine scenes, and the second section is meant to be an Alpine storm.

Students' reactions are very varied. In general they hear pastoral scenes for the first and third sections but they often hear the second as a cityscape. One of David's colleagues asked to borrow a cassette as a follow-up to work on describing places and David lent her this overture. She returned the cassette with a note: 'Went down a treat!'

RIVERS

I wish I could help you, but it must be cultural, you know. I can't see anything with your music . . . This music just makes me think of water running from a spring.

A Vietnamese listening to the beginning of *Vltava*

This activity exploits the highly descriptive music of Smetana's overture *Vltava (Die Moldau)* from *Má vlast*, which describes a river from its source to its end. The students imagine and describe the scenes it passes.

Preparation

If you have an OHP, prepare a transparency with the prompts for Step 5.

Procedure

1 Elicit from your students the names of major British rivers and add as you feel appropriate. Include Thames, Severn, Avon, Mersey, Tyne, Forth, Clyde. If you are British and feel strongly about your local river, add that too. Do the same for major European rivers, especially those few that have anglicised names: Rhine, Danube, Tiber, Tagus, Elbe, Volga, again adding others that you feel are important. You may also want to add major world rivers: Nile, Amazon, Ganges, Mississippi, etc.

2 Put your students into pairs and ask them to write down any words they associate in any way with rivers. Elicit these words and on the board put them into groups that are connected, e.g. types and stages

6.2

LEVEL
Intermediate +

TIME
35–80 minutes

FOCUS
Vocabulary relating to rivers; Writing; Reading; Listening

EXTRAS
An OHP and transparency (optional)

of rivers (*spring, stream, estuary, delta, mouth*), features of rivers (*waterfall, rapids, meander, island*), plants and creatures (*fish, dragonflies, ducks, swans, reeds, bulrushes, willows*), scenery (*marsh, valley, ravine*), human intervention (*locks, boats, landing-stage*). Add any items you feel they should learn. Ask them for verbs to describe the movement of water in rivers. Write them on the board and again add any extra ones you consider important. Your list might include: *trickle, flow, rush, swirl, lap.*

3 Tell the class they are going to listen to a piece of music that describes the River Vltava (Moldau) in Czechoslovakia from its source to its end, where it enters the River Elbe. As they listen to the music they are to write brief notes about each scene they hear. Emphasise that they should write very little at this stage because they will have an opportunity to expand their notes later.

4 Play Smetana's *Vltava.*

5 Put the class into groups of four and ask them to describe to each other the scenes they imagined the river passing. Then ask them to expand their notes into a series of descriptions of the river in its different stages. Project these prompts with an OHP or write them on the board as a guide.

I heard . . .
The scene then passed to . . .
After that I heard a change of scene to . . .
After a while I thought I heard . . .
At that point I'm sure I heard . . .

Your students may want to hear the music again before or during this stage. Play it again, but remember it will take about twelve minutes.

6 As your students finish, encourage them to exchange their versions. Ask them to give each other suggestions for improvements in the language (correcting errors, suggesting better turns of phrase).

7 Smetana gave an explicit account of what he was trying to describe. Read it to your class. Discuss with them how similar this is to their own descriptions.

The work depicts the course of the Vltava, beginning from the two small sources, the cold and warm Vltava, the joining of both streams into one, then the flow of the Vltava through forests and across meadows, through the countryside where joyful festivals are just being celebrated; by the light of the moon a dance of water nymphs; on the nearby cliffs proud castles, mansions and ruins rise up; the Vltava swirls in the St John's rapids, flows in a broad stream as far as Prague, the Vyšehrad appears, and finally the river disappears in the distance as it flows majestically into the Elbe.
(From J. Clapham's book *Smetana*)

VARIATION
Instead of Steps 5 and 6, ask your class to write the fuller version for homework. This has the advantage of allowing for a more thoughtful final written version, but the disadvantage of losing immediacy.

NOTE

Here is an (uncorrected) example of how one student heard the music (a version done as homework):

I first hear what seems to be the spring of a river, between the green mountains – transparent water running through the rocks with all the strenght of someone who has just born. Dragon flies fly from side to side, which is covered with moss.

Gradually, it becomes a stream and, from time to time, I can imagine sumptuous waterfalls. Both banks of the river are now fulled of willow whose hanging twigs dive in the river.

Next scene shows us the 'civilisation' – boats, sailors, fishermen flotting on the river, trying too lead their lives. In contrast with this tension, there are the ruins of primitive water-mills.

After a while I think I hear a warning. It is shouting danger and I can imagine factories polluting the river. Water becomes dark dam. The life of the river dies.

At last I hear the triumphal arrival of the river at the Ocean. This is the end of its tiring way. It finally reaches its goal the Ocean.

(Sofia, 16)

ACKNOWLEDGEMENT
Smetana's description of the Vltava is taken from Clapham (1972:77).

PASTORAL SCENES Constable meets Beethoven

In this activity we bring together music and paintings (or photographs) as stimuli for work on describing landscapes. We exemplify this with Beethoven's 'Pastoral' Symphony (No. 6) and Constable's paintings.

Preparation

Gather three or four photos or, preferably, paintings of contrasting landscapes per six to twelve students (maximum nine if you have only three pictures). Each group needs a set of the same pictures, so if you have a class of more than twelve you will need two or three copies of each picture. Good examples of paintings to use are the following ones by John Constable (they are obtainable as postcards from the addresses given).

The Cornfield reproduced by permission of the National Gallery, Trafalgar Square, London WC2N 5DN

The Cottage in a Cornfield and *Detail of the Valley of the Stour* reproduced by permission of the Victoria and Albert Museum, Cromwell Road, London SW7 2RL

Hampstead Heath with a Rainbow reproduced by permission of the Tate Gallery, Millbank, London SW1P 2RL

Museums and art galleries, in general, are a good source of visuals for this activity.

6.3

LEVEL
Intermediate +

TIME
50–80 minutes

FOCUS
Describing landscapes; Vocabulary; The four main skills

EXTRAS
3 or 4 colour pictures of landscapes per 6–12 students

Fig. 12a The Cornfield

Fig. 12b The Cottage in a Cornfield

Fig. 12c Detail of the Valley of the Stour

Fig. 12d Hampstead Heath with a Rainbow

Procedure

1 Divide the class into groups of six to twelve students and further sub-divide these into pairs or groups of three. Give each pair/three a picture and ask them to write down vocabulary to describe the picture in terms of what you can see, hear and smell – a list for each sense. Give them a time limit of five minutes. At the end of this time, ask them to write a sentence saying how they would feel if they were in the picture. Then within the larger groups (of six to twelve) get each pair/three to pass on their picture to another pair/three. The pairs/threes repeat the process of writing down vocabulary and the 'How would you feel?' sentence for each of the remaining pictures. It is important not to let your students spend more than five minutes on each picture, otherwise this first part of the lesson will become very monotonous. While the students are thinking and writing, play the second movement of Beethoven's 'Pastoral' Symphony quietly in the background. This will help to get them going. It lasts about ten minutes, after which they will be in the swing of things and you needn't play any more.

2 Ask the students within each larger group to report to one another the words they wrote down for each picture to add to their own lists. Ask them to discuss within the larger group how they think they would feel in each picture.

3 Tell your students to put the pictures on a desk where all from their group can see them. Then tell them you are going to play them a short excerpt of music which describes a landscape. Which picture do they most associate with the music and why? Play about two minutes of the opening of the fifth movement of Beethoven's 'Pastoral' Symphony.

4 Ask your students for their reactions. We have found that there is by no means agreement as to which picture they associate with the music, but that those who choose the same picture usually do so for similar reasons.

5 Tell the class what the music was. Inform them that Beethoven was greatly inspired by the countryside and often used to go out of the city for a walk with his music sketchbook, to write down ideas. Tell them that you are now going to play another movement and that you want them, as they listen, to write a description of the scene they imagine Beethoven was looking at as he wrote down the ideas for this music. Play the whole of the first movement. If needed, allow them a little time to finish after hearing the music. Ask them to pass round their descriptions so that everyone in their group can read them.

Here is an uncorrected example of what one student wrote:

I see a small village, surrounded by trees. The houses are small and the streets are narrow. Some people are talking in the street and a waggon, pulled by two cows, is passing slowly.

The sky is deep blue, with no clouds, and the sun is shining. It's warm and peaceful.

Some birds are singing in the trees, while others are flying over the village. A child is giving pieces of bread to the ducks in a lake. Near by other children are playing in the street.

(Isabel, 21)

OTHER SUGGESTED MUSIC

As well as Beethoven's 'Pastoral' Symphony, there are pastoral movements in a number of Baroque concertos and Handel's *Messiah*. Vaughan Williams also wrote a *Pastoral Symphony* (No. 3) and Lars-Erik Larsson a *Pastoral Suite*, Op. 19.

VARIATION

Select pictures of different kinds of seascapes (including different weathers) and select music describing the sea. Otherwise follow the same procedures as above. There are a number of impressive seascapes by Turner. For music you could try Debussy's *La Mer* or Britten's 'Sea Interludes' from the opera *Peter Grimes* (there are many recordings available separately from the opera).

SEASONS AND TIMES OF DAY

Procedure

SEASONS

1 Ask your class to think of the seasons of the year. What kind of things are affected by the change in season? Elicit such things as the weather, the length of the day, the kind of light in the sky, the landscape, vegetation, animals and birds, people's mood.

2 Divide the class into groups of four. Tell them you want one person in each group to work on one of the four seasons – spring, summer, autumn, winter – and write down what they associate with their season. Give them a time limit of five minutes.

3 Tell them to take turns to read the associations they've written to the others in their group. Ask the others to add anything they think has been left out.

4 Tell the class you are going to play them a piece of music which describes one of the seasons. Ask them to decide which season they think it is and why.

5 Play the music.

6 Ask the students to discuss their reactions within their group of four. Then open it up into a general class discussion.

EXTENSION

Set a composition with the title 'If you were a season of the year, which would you choose to be and why?'

6.4

LEVEL
Intermediate +

TIME
20–30 minutes

FOCUS
Vocabulary relating to seasons/times of day; Speaking; Extension – Writing

EXTRAS
None

SUGGESTED MUSIC

1 Vivaldi: 'The Four Seasons'. Use any movement you find evocative. We would particularly recommend the second movement of 'Winter'.
2 You could also explore Glazunov's ballet *The Seasons*, especially Variation 2, 'La Glace' ('Ice') of 'Winter', where the 'sound of ice' is very effectively created through the use of the glockenspiel.

TIMES OF DAY

Follow the same kind of procedure as with seasons.

1 Ask your class to tell you how they feel at different times of the day. Which time of day do they like best?
2 Divide the class into groups of four. Tell them you want one person in each group to work on one of the times of day – sunrise and morning, midday and afternoon, sunset and dusk, evening and night – and write down what they associate with their time of day. Give them a time limit of five minutes.
3 Follow Steps 3–6 as above, but for times of day.

EXTENSION

Set a composition with the title 'If you were a time of day, which would you choose to be and why?'

SUGGESTED MUSIC

Morning

1 Elgar: *Chanson de matin*
2 Grieg: 'Morning' from *Peer Gynt*
3 Haydn: Symphony No. 6 ('Le matin')
4 Strauss, Johann (younger): 'Morning Papers' ('Morgenblätter')

Afternoon

1 Haydn: Symphony No. 7 ('Le midi')
2 Debussy: *Prélude à l'après-midi d'un faune*

Evening and night

1 Bartók: Music for Strings, Percussion and Celesta, third movement, especially the central section
2 Beethoven: Piano Sonata in C sharp minor No. 14, Op. 27 No. 2, ('Moonlight'/'Mondschein'), first movement
3 Elgar: *Chanson de nuit*
4 Haydn: Symphony No. 8 ('Le soir')
5 Mozart: *Eine kleine Nachtmusik*, K 525
6 Schoenberg: *Verklärte Nacht*, especially the last part

WEATHER

For this activity we are taking Mertz's guitar piece 'La rimembranza' by way of example.

Procedure

1 Write the word *weather* in the middle of the board and five lines radiating from it. At the end of these lines write the basic weather words: *temperature, sunshine, rain, snow, cloud, wind.* Ask your students for more words and phrases related to these, either describing them in more detail or associated with them. Add these to the board radiating from the basic words. Your board will look something like this:

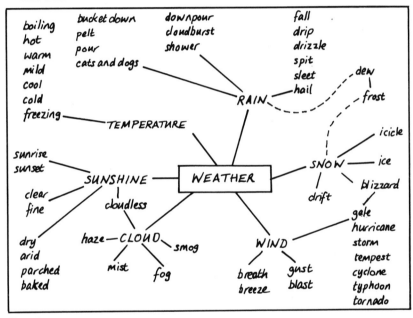

Fig. 13

2 Ask your students to describe the day's weather in detail, as it appears looking out through the window.
3 Tell them you are going to play them a piece of music. Ask them, as they listen, to imagine a scene and especially the weather in it. Play the music.
4 Divide the class into groups of five or six and ask them to tell each other about the scene and weather they visualised.

   David told one of his classes that when he hears this music he imagines himself looking out from an upstairs window:

There is a wooden veranda outside. It's raining steadily, drips fall from the roof onto the wooden veranda railing. The sky is grey. Eventually the rain ceases and a few people begin to venture out. The sky remains grey and it begins to rain again, then stops again. It goes on raining intermittently. Only at the end does the sun come out.

6.5

LEVEL
Intermediate +

TIME
25–40 minutes

FOCUS
Weather
vocabulary;
Speaking; Listening

EXTRAS
None

David's students had varied reactions. Here is an unedited transcript of what they said:

I agree . . . I imagine . . . Listening to the music I imagine wet streets, rain . . . I don't know if we can say 'naked trees' . . . umbrellas, people with raincoats, something to do with winter and rain . . .

(Madalena, 22)

I don't agree so much . . . it seems like in summer to autumn because it seemed it was going to rain but . . . but . . . it was . . . we could feel the summer because . . . like if the leaves were falling from the trees and something like that, but not raining . . . maybe almost like to rain . . . between summer and autumn . . .

(Rita, 17)

I identify this music with autumn too. The image I get, visualising, was of a great park . . . It was dawn, about 6 a.m. and there was no one there. The trees were . . . the leaves were falling from . . . they were not falling, they were already on the ground and . . . and they were being pushed by the wind across the park and a, how do you say? a brown image . . . and as the music continued sometimes the wind would . . . slow down and sometimes it would get stronger but not too stronger and by . . . at the end of the music I imagine that . . . people were starting to pass through the park, not many people, a few joggers, just a few, one or two, some . . . someone, I don't know who is, who was, and just . . . there was no rain, just the wind, smooth and . . . and that's it.

(Susana, 19)

OTHER SUGGESTED MUSIC

Khatchaturian: Piano Concerto, second movement. Most people hear late autumn with grey skies or winter scenes with snow and ice.

VARIATION

Storms

Follow the same procedure as above but make *storm* your central word and elicit/provide storm-related vocabulary. Your board might look something like this:

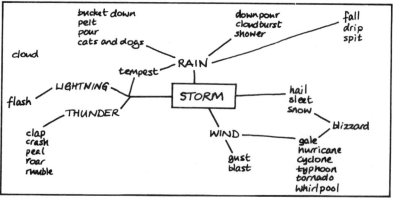

Fig. 14

There are many musical storms. The best is probably:
Rossini: Overture to *William Tell*, second section
There are also musical storms in Rossini's operas *The Barber of Seville* and *La Cenerentola*, but these are more stylised.

THE MUSIC OF NATURE

Preparation

1 During a lesson take five to ten minutes to ask your students for examples of natural music. Write them on the board. You can expect your class to come up with bird songs, the sound of the wind, of waves, of water running, leaves rustling, insects chirping or buzzing and cats purring.
2 Ask your students to pay attention to the natural music they hear in their lives and to come and report on this in a later lesson. Encourage them to record some of this music and to bring it to class in a later lesson. Also ask your students if they can bring in man-made music that reminds them of natural music. Prepare some selections of both kinds of music yourself.

Procedure

1 In a later lesson put your students in groups of four to talk about the natural music in their lives. Appoint a secretary for each group to report to the class. Allow five to ten minutes for this.
2 Ask the secretaries in each group to report to the class.
3 Play some of the recordings brought in by your students or by yourself and ask the class to identify them. Ask the students who brought them in to explain when and where they heard this music. Invite the class to comment and to say what effect this natural music has on them, and what they associate it with. Allow ten to fifteen minutes for this.

We often hear comments such as:

On my way to school I pass near a small square with trees and if I pass there when the sun is beginning to rise, I hear a concert of birds singing in the trees. I have come to look forward to this. I am very disappointed when the birds do not sing because the weather is too bad.

When I study in summer I hear birds singing. In the evening there is a blackbird that always sings on the roof.

I just love watching TV with my cat purring on my lap. I feel I am really at home.

I hate the croaking of the toads at night in the brook near my house.

4 Explain to your students that you are going to play musical excerpts that you or other students associate with natural music, and tell them

6.6

LEVEL
Intermediate +

TIME
40–50 minutes

FOCUS
Vocabulary of natural music;
Speaking;
Listening;
Extension: Writing poems

EXTRAS
Recordings of natural music

to listen and to write down what natural music they associate the excerpts with. Help your students to concentrate (Activity 1.1 *Focusing* is appropriate here – choose a green or a light blue colour). Play two or three short musical excerpts selected by your students or yourself and that you or your students associate with natural music.

5 Ask your students to compare their impressions in their groups of four and to discuss in what ways they feel the music composed by musicians is superior or inferior to the music of nature. The secretary reports to the class.

VARIATION

If some natural music can be heard in the classroom (birds singing in trees near the classroom, a brook running nearby, etc.), start from that natural music for your lesson.

EXTENSIONS

Invite your students to write and record a poem or a poetical composition about topics such as:

- The music of nature
- The music of the forest
- The music of the sea
- The music in my garden
- The music in the playground
- The music of the fields
- The music on my way to school
- Life without the sounds of nature etc.

  Encourage your students to illustrate these works with recorded samples of natural music related to the topic, or with music they associate with it. Some of our students have also illustrated their works with drawings.

SUGGESTED MUSIC

1 A lot of New Age music refers to nature. Kitaro's *Ki* also has interesting passages.
2 Debussy: *La Mer*
3 Vaughan Williams: *The Lark Ascending*
4 Delius: *On Hearing the First Cuckoo in Spring*
5 Delius: *A Song before Sunrise*
6 Vaughan Williams: *The Wasps*
7 Elgar: *Chanson de matin*
8 Rimsky-Korsakov: 'The Flight of the Bumblebee' from *Tsar Sultan*

CHAPTER 7

Topics

The activities in this chapter focus on four main topics: colours, advertising, rooms and leisure activities. We have exploited the links between the topic and music in a variety of ways.

COLOURS

Many people associate colours with other things in life that have nothing obviously to do with colour, e.g. days of the week and people's character. We find that our students need little encouragement to associate colour and music.

Preparation

Select three short contrasting musical excerpts (between ten and thirty seconds each) that suggest colours to you.

Procedure

1 Elicit from your students the names of colours. At beginner level it may help to bring objects of various colours into class and ask what colour they are. At intermediate level upwards it is best simply to ask the class for the names of colours and list these on the board as they say them. Then get them to process this list in one of the following ways:
   - Ask them to put the colours in two different orders – the order of colours in a rainbow and the continuum black to white.
   - Take, say, ten colours and ask your students to rank these in order of preference. Then put them into pairs and ask them to compare their order and discuss the differences.
   - Ask your students to decide which colour in the list on the board they most like to have around them and then think of three things that are just that colour. Tell them to write a sentence mentioning the three objects but without naming the colour; they mustn't let other students see what they have written. When they are ready, ask them to read out their sentences to the others in the class (divided into smaller groups if the class is very big), who have to guess what the colour is.
2 Tell the class you are going to play them three short musical excerpts and that you would like them to say what colour they 'see' or associate with the music as they listen. Tell them not to think too hard but just try and let a colour come to mind. Play the first excerpt. Then ask them what colour the music evoked. At intermediate level upwards ask them to try and explain why they chose that colour. If

7.1

LEVEL
Elementary +

TIME
10–40 minutes, depending on level of students

FOCUS
Names of colours; Giving explanations; The four main skills

EXTRAS
None

you have a large class, it is best to divide it into groups of four or five and ask them to tell one another the colour they heard and their explanation. Repeat this process with the second and third excerpts.

EXTENSION

Follow up with further discussion on colours and their associations. Start with obvious things such as colour and objects, e.g. green and vegetation, blue and sky, purple and royalty. Suggest that some people also associate colours with less obvious things, e.g. days of the week. See if anyone in your class associates colours with anything unusual.

SUGGESTED MUSIC

On the cassette you will find:

1 Vivaldi: Piccolo Concerto (*Concerto per flautino*) in C, PV 79/RV 443, opening of the first movement (version for recorders). This tends to evoke a broad range of light colours, especially blue and gold.

2 Handel: Organ Concerto No. 4 in F, opening of the first movement. Again a range of light colours, especially green and white.

3 Mahler: Symphony No. 1 in D minor, opening of the fourth movement. Almost everyone chooses red or black (dark grey).

You can use almost any music. Baroque music, especially in major keys tends to evoke light colours, whereas Romantic music, especially Brahms, Bruckner and Sibelius, tends to evoke much more sombre colours.

7.2

LEVEL
Intermediate +

TIME
40–50 minutes in Lesson 1, more time during later lessons

FOCUS
Vocabulary of persuasion; Oral fluency; Writing

EXTRAS
A selection of different kinds of music; index cards; video-recording equipment (optional)

MUSIC AND ADVERTISING

Preparation

1 Ask your students, at least a week in advance, to pay particular attention to commercials on TV and to find commercials for which the music is particularly well chosen. Tell them you will expect them to be able to describe the commercials and to explain why the music suits the advertisements.

2 Choose a number of products for which you want your students to create a TV commercial. Prepare descriptions on index cards. Have a mixture of serious, businesslike descriptions and more surrealistic ones (see page 88).

3 Have short selections of music (three minutes each) available for your students.

Procedure

1 Put your students into groups of four. Ask them to discuss which TV commercials they have seen recently that have stuck in their mind because of their music. Appoint one person in each group of four to explain the views of the group about the appropriacy of the music to the class afterwards. The class should come to the conclusion that

what matters are the links between:
- the music and the style of the commercial
- the music and the product
- the music and the image of the product.

Another point would be the catchiness of the tune. It should be easy to remember and easy to associate with the product.

2 Explain to your students they are going to create a commercial in groups of four. Some music is at their disposal but they will be able to collect more material and music to finish the advertisement after class. If you can record their commercials on videotape, tell them you are going to do this, and that a jury will award prizes afterwards.

3 Hand out your index cards with descriptions of products to each group. Each group then decides which product they are going to advertise. If they do not find a product that catches their fancy, they can invent a product themselves.

4 Tell the groups to prepare their commercial. They need to: agree on a slogan, write the script for their sketch, decide what music they want, make a list of additional material they will need, decide who is going to look for what. Help them out in any way required while they do this.

5 In a later lesson, have each group present its commercial to the class. The class awards a prize. You can have several categories, such as:
- the most honest commercial
- the most colourful commercial
- the zaniest commercial
- the best music
- the most original commercial
- the best acting
- the most memorable commercial

If your school has an audio-visual studio, get the groups to record their commercials on video tape. They can then view their commercials on TV in class. This allows you to show the commercials to other classes as well as to have an independent jury to award the prizes.

6 Round off this activity with a discussion on standards in advertising.

EXTENSION 1

Students write a text to explain why they find the commercial that obtained the highest number of votes is the best or why they think it is not. You can impose a format for the text, such as an internal memorandum for a company, a formal report, a letter to an advertising agency to complain about a commercial or to reject it.

EXTENSION 2

Composition: 'Commercials in our life' or 'For or against commercials'.

VARIATION 1

If your students are training to work in business, ask them to analyse the commercials in more professional terms such as:
- How far do the advertisers manage to come up with a Unique Selling Proposition (USP)?

- Do the commercials meet the requirements of the usual four stages for promoting a product ('AIDA'):

  i attract the *Attention* of potential customers

  ii arouse the *Interest* of potential customers in the product

  iii create a *Desire* for the product

  iv persuade the potential customer to take prompt *Action*.

Ask your students to find ways of attracting the attention, arousing the interest, creating a desire for the product and of compelling potential customers to take prompt action.

VARIATION 2

Invite your students to make a commercial about their school, their village, etc. or themselves. Encourage those who can play an instrument to play the music themselves and even to compose it if they can.

Example product descriptions:

1 This is a new pasta. Its distinguishing feature is the shapes it comes in. There are animal shapes, leaf shapes and flower shapes.

2 The product you have to advertise is a dog exerciser. The aim is to make dogs more athletic and less fat and to allow dog owners to stay indoors when the weather is bad. (*With thanks to Alan Hirvela for the idea – Hirvela 1987.*)

3 This is the ultimate in fly catching. Not an insecticide: it's a computerised mini-rocket that kills each fly individually. The rockets are re-usable.

4 To combat pollution in cities a four-wheeled vehicle driven by pedals. The riders are kept dry and warm.

5 A silencer. This device will stop Walkmans from playing in trains and buses.

6 A service to provide wailers and weepers at funerals.

7 An extraordinary washing powder: it washes whiter, makes your washing smell better and is phosphate free. After washing your clothes, you can use the water to fertilise your garden.

8 A new service to all: we write Christmas cards by hand for all busy people.

SOME MUSIC YOUR STUDENTS COULD USE

1 Bizet: *Carmen*, several arias such as 'Flower Song', 'Smugglers' chorus', 'Carmen chorus' ('L'amour est un oiseau rebelle')

2 Sarasate: *Carmen Fantaisie*, Op. 25. The different movements can be used for different kinds of advertisements.

3 Sarasate: 'Habañera'

4 Field: Nocturne No. 4

5 Verdi: 'Chorus of the Hebrew Slaves' ('Va pensiero') from *Nabucco*

6 Gounod: 'Soldiers' chorus' ('Gloire Immortelle'), from *Faust*

7 Beethoven: Piano Sonata in C sharp minor No. 14, Op. 27 No. 2 'Moonlight' ('Mondschein'), first movement

8 J.S. Bach: Air from Orchestral Suite No. 3 in G major, BWV 1068

ACKNOWLEDGEMENT

We found the criteria for analysing commercials in Jones and Alexander (1989).

ROOMS

This activity requires students to describe rooms with considerable precision. It also encourages imagination. If you are restricted to fifty-minute lessons, do up to the end of Step 3 in one lesson and continue from Step 4 in the next.

Procedure

1 Ask your students to imagine they have to describe the room they are in to someone who is blind. Put them in pairs to write a description of the room. Tell them to ask you for any vocabulary they need. Set a time limit of fifteen minutes.

2 After the fifteen minutes ask each pair to exchange their description with another pair. Tell them to write on the description they receive the word *expand* wherever they feel a blind person would not be clear as to what they meant. Then they give the descriptions back to the writers for them to expand their descriptions as required. Allow a further five minutes for this.

3 Tell the students that the purpose of the exercise they have just done is to make them attentive to detail when describing a room. Now with similar detail, they must write individually a description of a room they particularly like. Explain that it could be their own room at home, or it could be some other. If done in class, allow twenty minutes for this, again supplying vocabulary as needed. Alternatively, this could be set for homework to be brought to class next day.

4 Put the students into pairs. Ask them to exchange descriptions of the room they particularly like and to read their partner's description. Tell them to ask their partner to clarify anything they don't under-stand and explain why they like the room so much.

5 Ask the class as a whole what kind of room they like to be in when they are trying to do their homework or other 'brain work'. What features in the room are important to them? Now tell them you are going to play a piece of music. Ask them as they listen to write down a brief description of the room they imagine the composer was in while he was composing the music. Do a brief concentration activity, e.g. Activity 1.2 *Follow the Spiral*, Variation 3.

6 Play the music (three or four minutes). Put the class into groups of four to six students to discuss the rooms they heard.

SUGGESTED MUSIC

Any extract lasting three or four minutes, but preferably by a composer whose 'work room' you are in a position to tell the students about, e.g. Stravinsky, Rossini or Wagner (see Notes below). Try, for example, an excerpt from:

1 Stravinsky: *Pulcinella*
2 Stravinsky: *Oedipus Rex*
3 Rossini: Overture to *The Thieving Magpie (La gazza ladra)*
4 Rossini: any of the late piano pieces, e.g. from *Péchés de ma vieillesse*, or in the orchestral version by Britten as *La Boutique Fantasque*.

7.3

LEVEL
Intermediate +

TIME
50–70 minutes

FOCUS
Describing rooms;
Writing; Reading

EXTRAS
None

5 Wagner: *Parsifal* or *Lohengrin*, opening of the Prelude

6 Wagner: *Siegfried Idyll*

NOTES

The Dynamics of Creation (Storr 1976, Chapter 8) cites three examples of the rooms in which composers worked:

1 Stravinsky

His Hollywood studio was meticulously laid out with two pianos (a grand and an upright), two desks (an elegant writing desk and a draftsman's desk), two cupboards with glass shelves (for his books, scores and sheet music, all in alphabetical order), a couch for his afternoon nap, a number of small tables (one with all a smoker could ask for) and about half a dozen chairs.

2 Rossini

In his latter years in Paris he always worked in his bedroom (as he had tended to do all his life), where he also received guests. In the centre was a table with all his writing equipment neatly laid out. Four wigs were in a row on the mantelpiece, Japanese miniatures on the white walls, an oriental object on the chest of drawers. His bed was carefully made.

3 Wagner

In his latter years, in particular, needed to be in a room where he was surrounded by pastel colours and soft fabrics, such as velvet, silk, satin.

ACKNOWLEDGEMENT

Reading about composers and their rooms in Storr's book gave us the idea for this activity.

7.4

LEVEL
Intermediate +

TIME
30–40 minutes

FOCUS
Vocabulary of streams and fish; Listening for content; Dialogue writing; Discussion

EXTRAS
None

FISHING

This activity exploits Satie's 'La pêche' (▭) from *Sports et divertissements* and encourages students to use their imagination.

Procedure

1 Set the scene. Tell your students to imagine a stream. Ask them to write down vocabulary describing the sound and movement of the water. When you sense they are ready, ask them to read out their words. Here are some that one class wrote: *splash, running, calm, soft, quick, silence, roar, troubled, singing, dancing*. At a more advanced level you could add expressions such as *babbling brook, gurgling, murmuring, rushing torrents*.

Now tell them to imagine the bottom of the stream. Tell them to write down words describing that too. When they're ready ask them again for their words. The same class gave these: *sand, stones, rocky, frogs, waterweed, gravel*. You may want to add *mud* and *pebbles*. Now tell them to imagine one fish meeting two others. Ask them to write words to describe fish. The class may well not know the English words for parts of the fish's body, e.g. *fins*, *scales*, *gills*, in which case ask them to describe the things in terms of their function, where on the fish they are found, etc., so that you can provide the words.

2 Tell your students to imagine the conversation the fish might have. These fish speak English, of course! Put the students into pairs or threes to write down the conversation as a short dialogue (about ten lines). Give a time limit of ten minutes. After the ten minutes, ask the pairs (threes) to read out their dialogues. This gives the others in the room an idea of other possible conversations. Optionally, you may correct some of the errors after each dialogue has been read, but peer correction is not appropriate as the students should be listening to the content.

We have found that writing the dialogue between the fish really sets off the students' imaginations and there is a lot of laughter as they are writing. Here is a dialogue (uncorrected) that one group of three wrote:

A   Hello!
B   Hello!
C   Hello!
A   It's too wet, I'm catching a cold.
B   Did you see that silly golden fish?
C   I met her last storm.
A   I also met her, and she was afraid that the storm could mess her scales.
B   By the way, did you see her boyfriend?
C   Yes, he is a pretty fish! And he is letting his scales grow.
A   Bye!
B   Bye!
C   Bye!

(Ida, Zé and Sandra)

3 Tell the class that you are going to play them a very short piece of music, which begins by describing the bottom of a stream, one fish meeting two others and their conversation. Ask them as they listen to try and decide individually what the conversation is about. Play the music. Play it a second time if the students feel they want to hear it again.

4 Ask your students to discuss briefly with their partner(s) what they think they heard. Have a general discussion of what everyone heard.

NOTES

According to Erik Satie, what happens in the piece is that a fish at the bottom of a murmuring stream has spotted a poor fisherman. Two other fish come along and ask what's wrong. The fish tells them, they thank him, and all of the fish swim away home. Soon the fisherman goes home too, leaving the murmuring stream behind.

Satie's imagination was more vivid and bizarre than most people's, so don't expect your students to follow this storyline. However, the following is what two students heard:

There's a happy younger fish and two older fish who are not very happy. They have a row about the younger one's behaviour.

A big fish meets a little fish and wants to eat it, but when the big fish sees the little one's face it thinks that the little fish is so cute that it changes its mind.

7.5

LEVEL
Intermediate

TIME
25–45 minutes

FOCUS
Picnic vocabulary;
Speaking

EXTRAS
OHP and
transparency, or
multiple copies of
the list of food and
drink

PICNICS

In this activity the students discuss picnic food and drink before listening to Satie's 'Le pique-nique' from (🔲) *Sports et divertissements*.

Preparation

Put the list of cold foods and drinks below onto an OHP transparency or make a class set to hand out. (If any of the foods or drinks are taboo where you teach, omit or replace them by others.)

soup	mayonnaise	lettuce	grapes
chicken	butter	cucumber	peaches
ham	bread	tomatoes	tea
veal	cream crackers	cress	coffee
beef	cold rice	onion	milk
sausage	cake	bananas	water
tinned sardines	cream cakes	apples	wine
tinned tuna	chocolate	pears	beer
pâté	biscuits	cherries	lemonade
hard-boiled eggs	yoghurt	oranges	fruit juice

© Longman Group UK Ltd. 1992

Procedure

1 Introduce the subject of picnics. Where do your students like to go for picnics? Who do they go with? What's the best food to take?

2 Project the transparency or distribute the handouts. Go through the list and check that they know the vocabulary. Put the class into pairs. As a pair they must choose any eight items on the list to take on a picnic. They can choose other items not on the list so long as the total number of items is no more than eight.
Note: sandwiches count as two items (bread + contents) or three if with butter; chocolate biscuits count as two items (chocolate + biscuits).

3 Put the pairs into groups of four. They must again come to a consensus over the eight items. Then put the fours into eights to repeat the process. The eights into sixteens, the sixteens into a whole class. (Reduce the number of stages if you find boredom setting in, but always include the whole class consensus.)

4 Elicit from the class what kind of things can spoil a picnic, e.g. bad weather, noise, wasps, ants and other insects, too many people, dirt.

5 Tell your students you are going to play them a short piece of music that describes a picnic. Ask them what food they think the picnickers took with them and what spoilt the picnic. Play the music. If you think they want to hear it again, play it again.

6 Ask your students for their thoughts. When they have finished telling you, tell them that, according to the composer, everyone on the picnic took cold veal to eat but the picnic was brought to a halt by a storm.

EXTENSION

Organise a picnic with the class. Make sure that one or more students bring each of the eight items the class had decided on in Step 3. Other students can bring extras, including umbrellas, insect repellant or whatever other precautionary items are considered necessary.

HOLIDAYS

Preparation

Select three short recordings (each lasting two minutes) of different kinds of music that call to mind three different holiday atmospheres.

Procedure

1 Put your students into groups of four, and ask them to find three points their most recent holidays had in common. Also, ask them to decide who will speak for the group later. Help your students with any words they need and then ask them to write these on the board for the whole class to see. Allow ten minutes for this first activity.

2 Go through the vocabulary on the board with the whole class. Students take notes if they need to.

3 Ask one student in each group of four to explain to the class what points they have found they have in common.

4 Explain to the class that holiday experiences can be conveyed through music and that you are going to play three pieces of music. Explain you expect them to listen carefully to the three pieces and that you want them to decide which piece best corresponds to their ideal holidays and why. They will explain this to a partner.

5 Ask your students to close their eyes and to think of holidays.

6 Play the three excerpts.

7 Ask your students to picture the classroom in their minds and to slowly open their eyes.

8 Ask for a show of hands to find out which piece each student associates with ideal holidays, and, as far as possible, pair each student with one who has chosen a different piece. Invite your students to explain their choice to each other.

7.6

LEVEL
Intermediate +

TIME
About 30–40 minutes

FOCUS
Speaking;
Vocabulary;
Extension; Reading and writing

EXTRAS
Holiday brochures for the extension

EXTENSION 1

1 Ask your students to find some publicity in some travel holiday brochure or an advertisement from the leisure section of some newspaper that they feel broadly corresponds to their ideal holiday and bring it to class next time.

2 In the next lesson tell your students to exchange these with a partner and ask each student to try to deduce why their partner has chosen this particular holiday. They talk this over.

EXTENSION 2

If practicable, encourage your students to write a letter to a travel agency in which they describe their ideal holidays and ask for suggestions and brochures. When they have received an answer, the students come and report to the class on how far the offers made and the brochures received actually correspond to their wishes.

SUGGESTED MUSIC

Choose three different kinds of music that reflect the usual patterns that emerge when it comes to holidays. The first excerpt should be calm, the second incite to do things such as sport, the third stimulate desire to discover things and experience adventures.

For relaxing holidays

1 Albinoni: excerpt from any of the oboe concertos
2 Telemann: excerpts from any of the oboe concertos and quartets or recorder suites
3 Vivaldi: excerpts from the piccolo/recorder concertos
4 Beethoven: Symphony No. 6 ('Pastoral'), second movement.

For more active holidays

1 Mendelssohn: Symphony No. 3 in A minor, Op. 56 ('Scottish') third movement (Vivace non troppo)
2 Coates:
   a) *Meadow and Mayfair Suite:* 'Evening in Town' (Valse)
   b) 'The Dam Busters' (March)
3 Dvořák: Symphony No. 5 in F, Op. 76, opening of the first movement
4 Bizet: Symphony in C, first or fourth movement

For adventurous holidays

1 Britten: *The Prince of the Pagodas*, opening of Act III
2 Frank Martin: Études for String Orchestra, fourth movement (Pour le style fugué)
3 Chopin: Polonaise No. 6, Op. 54 in A flat ('Heroic')
4 Andean flute music

CHAPTER 8

Awareness

This chapter is concerned with awareness of many different kinds. Activity 8.1 *I can hear* involves raising awareness of the senses. This is followed by an activity that makes us more conscious of silence. Activity 8.3 *Draw the music* encourages students to understand themselves better by getting them to 'translate' what they hear in a piece of music into visual form and by talking about their 'drawing' to express this also in verbal form. Activity 8.4 *Music and loneliness* revolves around music's great power to express and touch deep feelings. Activity 8.5 *The music that I am* raises an awareness of the people in the room, including self.

I CAN HEAR

This activity develops musical awareness and awareness in general, which excludes nothing and heightens the intensity of experience, as opposed to concentration, which excludes most of the world from our lives. Make sure there will be no interference from sources of loud sound, especially the first time you do this kind of exercise.

Preparation

1 Prepare your classroom beforehand by putting five unusual objects in different places in the classroom. They should be clearly visible, but not displayed ostentatiously.
2 Find a suitable short piece of music as described below.
3 Here we give an example with Japanese music. We have chosen a well-known piece called 'Edo Lullaby' (on Nonesuch Explorers 972 072-2, for instance). The instruments used are a shakuhachi, bells, a shamisen, a biwa and two kotos. Before class, select thirty-second long excerpts with each of the five instruments playing separately first to teach your students the names of the instruments and to get them to distinguish the sound they make.

Procedure

1 Ask your students if they find it hard to concentrate, and what helps them to concentrate. Encourage them to come up with as many ideas as possible.
2 Next, ask if they realise that concentration is not the only attitude of mind that is useful. Ask them if they remember instances when they were concentrating so hard on a particular fact that some other important thing escaped their notice. Trigger reactions by telling a true personal anecdote, such as the one that follows:

8.1

LEVEL
Intermediate +

TIME
20–25 minutes

FOCUS
Practising *I can hear*, *sounds like*, *reminds me of*; Speaking; Learning to distinguish similar sounds

EXTRAS
None

One day I was concentrating so hard on the traffic lights, as I was crossing a street that, halfway to the other side of the road, I bumped into my wife, who I hadn't even noticed. She hadn't noticed me either.

3 Ask your students to write down, without looking round, what changes they have noticed in the classroom. (Usually, very few students notice your new objects.)

4 Ask your class to read out what they have written, and then point out what you have added to the classroom environment. Encourage your students to comment on the experience. If objects were not noticed, say that this is an example of lack of awareness, and that they will be trying to develop their awareness in the activity you have planned for today.

5 In class, explain to your students you have chosen Japanese music and that first they are going to hear each instrument separately, in order to learn the names and to be able to distinguish these instruments by the sound they make.

6 Play each instrument separately and ask your students to deduce what kind of instrument it is. Help your students with questions such as: 'Is it a large instrument? What is it made of? How is it played? etc.' Also write *sounds like* and *reminds me of* on the board.

They will probably guess right away that the shakuhachi is a wooden flute (it is actually a bamboo flute). They will probably think that the shamisen must be a small instrument with few strings, and that the biwa too is a string instrument, but that it must be larger than the shamisen. Students tend also easily to conclude that the koto must be even larger than the biwa.

Ask your students to compare each instrument they hear with instruments they know. You can expect the following quite valid approximations:

The shakuhachi sounds like a smallish wooden flute. The shamisen sounds somewhat like a banjo. The biwa sounds rather like a lute. The koto reminds me of a harp.[1]

[1]It is in fact more like a large zither.

When you are satisfied your students know the names and can distinguish the instruments, move to the next step.

7 Tell your students you are going to play music featuring several different instruments. Explain that you want them to try to be aware of all the instruments *at the same time*. To help them, you will point out what instruments they hear as they are listening.

8 Stand behind your students. Ask them to close their eyes, or dim the light or switch it off. A concentration exercise is very useful at this point, e.g. Activity 1.2 *Follow the spiral*, Variation 2, page 10.

9 Ask your students to listen, and then play the music. Speak slowly in a distinct but not very loud voice:

'Can you hear the shakuhachi? Listen to the shakuhachi. Can you also hear the bells? Listen to the bells and the shakuhachi. Can you hear the shamisen? Listen to the shamisen, the bells and the shakuhachi. Can you hear the koto, the shamisen, the bells and the shakuhachi? Can you hear the biwa, the shakuhachi, the bells, the koto and the shamisen?'

10 When the music has stopped, pause for a few seconds. Ask your class to imagine the classroom in their minds, and then to open their eyes. Ask your students if they managed to hear all the instruments at the same time. Allow your students to express their feelings and ideas. Then tell them they are going to try on their own – without you helping them.

11 Play the music again, and allow your students to build up their awareness of the instruments on their own, without you guiding them.

12 Now, combine visual and auditory elements, possibly feelings, and allow your students to speak when they are ready:

I can hear the violin, I can see the flower near the window, I can see Maria's hand on the desk, I can feel my feet in my shoes and I can hear someone walking outside.

13 Talk the experience over with your students.

VARIATION 1

Once your students know the exercise, begin straight away with Step 6. Just tell them they are going to do an awareness exercise.

VARIATION 2

In teacher training, this is an excellent first step to develop the trainees' awareness of:

i the difficulty in paying attention to several things at the same time (intonation, accentuation, phonology, morphology and syntax, for example)

ii the difficulty in distinguishing similar things (phonemes and allo-phones, for example); use similar instruments for this (all string instruments or all brass instruments, for example).

EXTENSION 1

Allow students to bring in their own music and to practise this with the class.

EXTENSION 2

In later lessons steer your students' attention towards each other and the class environment to develop their awareness of the class.

EXTENSION 3

Use this exercise to gradually help your students to appreciate the complexity of one kind of music versus other kinds.

EXTENSION 4

Use this activity to make your students aware of the variations on themes in the music. Draw their attention to the repetition and the development of the basic melody.

SUGGESTED MUSIC

Any music where several instruments and/or voices are used is suitable. If your students know very little about music, prepare excerpts with solo instruments first, and get them to identify these. Then play a piece where all the instruments are heard. The instruments should start one by one in your first exercise. At the beginning choose instruments that are readily recognisable, such as the piano, the flute, the violin, the trumpet and the double bass. The range can be extended later by having several string instruments or several wind instruments. Here are some examples with different kinds of music.

Electronic music

The following may be particularly attractive to young people both in Europe and Asia:

1 Kitaro: *Ki*; the beginning of 'Sun' and 'Endless Water'
2 A lot of New Age music is suitable.

Make sure your students know the vocabulary to speak about electronic instruments first, or ask them to describe the sounds.

African music

Lamine Konté: Several pieces from *The Kora of Senegal (La Kora du Sénégal* Arion CD ARN 64036) are suitable. In particular: 'Abaraka' (guitar, bass guitar, flute, percussion), 'Moussol' (voice, piano, guitar, bass guitar, percussion), 'Nagnol' (voice, balafon, guitar, percussion).

Classical music

Britten: *A Young Person's Guide to the Orchestra* is probably the most obvious work to use here.

Ask your students to find more music. The search in itself is rewarding.

Pop music

We have used music by Jethro Tull ('Aqualung', 'Minstrel in the Gallery', 'Bursting Out'), and Pink Floyd ('Meddle' in particular).

Here too, ask your students to find more music.

ACKNOWLEDGEMENT
Jean Auquier, Librarian of the Ecole Normale Fernand Hotyat at Morlanwelz, Belgium, drew our attention to the importance of awareness training.

SILENCE IN MUSIC

This activity is dedicated to a busker in the Brussels Underground, who was asking for money *for the silence*. It makes your students aware of the importance of silence in their lives and in music.

Preparation

1 Get a blank cassette.
2 Choose some appropriate pieces of music as described below.

Procedure

1 Ostentatiously set up your cassette recorder and put a blank cassette in it, without telling your students it is blank.
2 Get your students to concentrate deeply. Activity 1.2 *Follow the spiral* (Variation 1 or 2, page 10) would be best here. Ask your class to listen carefully and not to open their eyes before you tell them to.
3 Play the blank cassette for one minute, then, in a whisper, ask your students to picture the classroom in their minds and to slowly open their eyes.
4 Elicit your students' reactions by asking questions such as: 'How did you feel as you were listening to the silence?' Lead the conversation towards the place of silence in their lives: 'Do you, in general, prefer silence or the absence of silence?'
5 Explain to your students you would like them to make a list of situations where music and other sounds disturb them, and a second one with situations where they like or even need music and other sounds. Give them five minutes for this. Here is an example of what happened in a class.

I hate music:	Other sounds I hate:
In restaurants	A dentist's drill
Walkmans in public places	People interrupting me
Music coming from my neighboursMotorbikes	
Buskers in Underground carriages	Cars sounding their horns at night
	Airplanes
	The telephone ringing

I need music:	Other sounds I like:
When I want to concentrate	My canary singing
In church	My cat purring
To go to sleep at night	A mountain brook
To awake properly	Children's voices in the distance
When I am nervous	The kettle boiling in the morning
At parties	

6 Get your students to sit in groups of four, and ask them to talk about their list, explaining why, in what precise situations they have

8.2

LEVEL
Intermediate +

TIME
40–50 minutes

FOCUS
Speaking; Some writing

EXTRAS
A blank audiocassette

suffered or regularly suffer because of music and noise, and the contrary. Give them five to ten minutes for this.

7 Ask your students if they have ever thought of the importance of silence in music. They usually react with a puzzled or amused silence. Then give your students quotations about music and silence such as the ones here:

- from Jiddu Krishnamurti's *The Only Revolution*, (Gollancz 1973) p. 129

  The silence that music produces as you listen to it is the product of that music, induced by it. Silence isn't an experience; you know it only when it is over.

- Music is expensive noise.

Elicit reactions. Encourage your students to speak about the links they feel there are between music and silence. If this is met with an embarrassed silence, immediately move to Step 8.

8 Tell your students you would like them to listen to the silence in three pieces of music, not to the music. Explain that you expect them to decide which piece makes the greatest use of silence, and what feelings the silence in the music induces in them. Insist it is not a matter of being louder or softer, but that they should listen to the silent moments in the music.

9 Get your class to concentrate. We suggest Activity 1.2 *Follow the spiral* (Variation 2, page 10). It is essential that the students close their eyes. Play the three pieces you have prepared.

10 Wait for fifteen seconds when the music has stopped and, barely above a whisper, ask your students to picture the classroom in their minds and to slowly open their eyes.

11 Ask them to discuss the experience in their groups, and to appoint a 'secretary' for each group. Help them out with any language they need. They often need vocabulary to qualify the silence. Allow five to ten minutes for them to use dictionaries, ask around or check their notes.

12 Appoint a student to write the feelings of the class about the silence they have heard in the music as the group secretaries report back to the whole class. The class secretary reports to the whole class in this form:

	Most silent	Between Most and Least	Least Silent
Excerpt 1	12	7	0
Excerpt 2	3	7	7
Excerpt 3	0	5	12

You will find that the results are not always clear-cut, because some students cannot make up their minds, or because they feel two pieces are equally silent. Allow your students to explain their feelings about the silence in the music. Write them on the board. For example:

Excerpt 1:   oppressive, bored, frightening silence
Excerpt 2:   welcome, relaxing, concentrated silence
Excerpt 3:   not silent, suppresses the noise in my head, so induces silence

EXTENSION 1

Ask your students to listen to some of their favourite pieces of music at home and to listen to the silence. Tell them you will want them to bring the music in a later lesson, speak about their findings, play the music they have brought and to lead to an activity similar to the one above.

EXTENSION 2

As homework, ask your students to look up words and collocations in their dictionaries to try and describe kinds of silences. Dictionaries for collocations such as *The Word Finder* (Rodale 1947) are ideal for this kind of activity. In a later lesson you can discuss kinds of silences with the class. For example, the students can talk about the following kinds of silence:

meaningful silence	reproachful silence
embarrassed silence	mysterious silence
oppressive silence	magical silence
understanding silence	noisy silence
roaring silence	white silence

EXTENSION 3

At home, students read Heinrich Böll's short story 'Doctor Murke's Collected Silences' ('Doktor Murkes Gesammeltes Schweigen' Nelson 1989). In a later lesson, ask them if they have ever come across people like Doctor Murke and how they have dealt with them.

EXTENSION 4

Study Simon and Garfunkel's song 'The Sound of Silence'.

EXTENSION 5

Topics for essays:
- Music and silence in my life.
- 'You can't buy silence as you would buy good cheese. You can't cultivate it as you would a lovely plant. It doesn't come about by any activity of the mind or of the heart.' (Krishnamurti: *The Only Revolution*, p. 129)
- 'Silence is freedom, and freedom comes with the finality of complete order.' (Krishnamurti: *The Only Revolution*, p. 139)
- There is no music without silence.

SUGGESTED MUSIC

You need three pieces that approach silence differently, each of two minutes at most. We suggest you take one from each list below or find some that have struck you personally.

Oriental music

1 It has been said that Indian music is a music that brings out silence (Daumal 1970). In ragas, the first movement, the *alap* is probably the one that makes the most striking use of silence. Chose any raga that is suited to the time of the day. (A piece from Ustad Imrat Khan's *Rag Megh*, for instance on Edelweiss CD ED 1018.)

2 In Japanese music the shakuhachi and other bamboo flutes are played to make silence more striking.

Contemporary European music

In particular:

1 Ysaÿe: Six Sonatas for Solo Violin, Op. 27
2 Varèse: *The Desert (Le Désert)*
3 Friedrich Zehm: Serenade
4 Lekeu: Trio in C minor for Piano, Violin and Cello, excerpts from the second movement

Other music

1 Albinoni: Adagio for Organ and Strings
2 Nielsen: Fantasy Piece for Clarinet and Piano (1881)
3 Nielsen: Fantasy Pieces for Oboe and Piano, Op. 2
4 Arias by Rossini, Bellini, Donizetti and Verdi, which have a pause at the end of the orchestral introduction, e.g. 'La donna è mobile' from Verdi's *Rigoletto*

8.3

LEVEL
Intermediate +

TIME
20–30 minutes

FOCUS
Free speaking;
Comparing
musical, graphic
and verbal
expression

EXTRAS
Colour pencils,
biros or felt-tipped
markers

DRAW THE MUSIC

This activity typically results in student drawings which are remarkably personal. In one class the same music can generate drawings depicting a girl dancing on the beach, a forest with flowers, the orchestra – represented by a few strokes, the waves of the sea, a singer dancing on a stage or a man galloping on a horse. Even students who are convinced they 'cannot draw' make interesting contributions to the discussion.

Preparation

Choose a short piece of music that suggests some kind of movement.

Procedure

1 Explain that music has often been a source of inspiration for artists. Today they will be artists and they will allow a piece of music to inspire them to make a drawing.
2 Explain that first everyone needs to choose the colour(s) for their drawing. Ask your students to close their eyes while the music is playing.
3 When the music has stopped, ask everyone to say what colour(s) they saw. They then choose pencils, biros or felt-tipped markers to draw.

4 Explain that every artist has a very personal brush stroke and that the music will help them to find their own personal stroke. In their drawing, they will use the basic stroke that the music induces in each of them individually. So, if they feel this music as a succession of straight lines, their drawing will be made with straight lines. If the music feels like a succession of curves, they will draw with curves. If they perceive spirals, they will use spirals, etc. Draw some examples of the kinds of lines the music can inspire on the board.

Fig. 15

5 Ask your students to allow their hands to move to the tune and rhythm, while remaining seated. Tell them this movement determines the kind of stroke they will use after the second playing.

6 After the second playing, tell the students they are going to listen to the music again and that you want them to let their hands trace a broad general pattern. Meanwhile, they draw using the colour(s) they saw and their personal stroke. This time, everyone allows their hands to draw what the music suggests.

7 Ask if they would like to hear the piece again while completing their drawings. They can also check if the drawing really reflects the feelings that the music inspires in them.

8 Put your students in pairs to talk about their drawings. They ask each other questions and make any comments they like. They can also say in what ways they feel they have not been able to draw what they felt. Students change partners and do this again to improve their original performance and to hear another viewpoint.

9 Discuss the experience of translating feelings into music, words or drawings with the whole class. Ask your students which means of expression comes most naturally to them and why.

VARIATION 1

1 Instead of Steps 8 and 9 the students exchange their drawings (allow them to choose their partners). They briefly describe in writing in what ways they feel their partner's drawing is similar to theirs.

2 They exchange their sheets with comments, read them and talk it over.

VARIATION 2

1 Instead of Steps 8 and 9 your students exchange drawings and write questions about the drawing they have in front of them.

2 They then give the drawing with the questions back to the artists.

3 The artists answer the questions in writing.

4 After reading each other's answers the students discuss the experience.

VARIATION 3

1 Instead of Steps 8 and 9, the students exchange their drawings with a partner and try to put into words what the other has expressed.

2 Each student gives the drawing back to the artist together with their interpretation. They discuss each other's interpretations.

SUGGESTED MUSIC

1 Johann Strauss (junior): *Acceleration Waltz*, opening

2 Mussorgsky: 'Hopak' (from *Sorochinsky Fair*)

3 Paganini: Concerto for Violin and Orchestra No. 4 in D minor, opening of the fourth movement

4 Rameau: *Les Indes Galantes* (any of the livelier pieces)

5 Handel: *Water Music,* first movement

8.4

LEVEL
Intermediate +

TIME
30–50 minutes

FOCUS
Discussion

EXTRAS
None

MUSIC AND LONELINESS

In this activity we use music as a means of focusing on the causes and solutions of loneliness. We illustrate the technique with the cello solo that opens the aria 'Ella giammai m'amò' from Verdi's opera *Don Carlos* ([cassette]) and the second movement of Dvořák's String Quartet in F, Op. 96 ('The American'), though the use of a second piece is optional.

Loneliness is something very near the surface in a lot of people. In particular, students studying for longer periods away from home may feel it acutely as homesickness. This may be something that needs to be talked about in the class. At the same time you must feel able to handle any upset that this activity provokes. It is also very important to allow enough time to reach Step 6, so that the activity ends on a positive note.

Procedure

1 In the middle of the board write the word *loneliness* and put a box round it. Ask your students what causes loneliness. Encourage a variety of answers. Write their responses around the 'loneliness-box' on the the board.

2 Tell the class you are going to play a piece of music which describes someone's loneliness. Ask them to try to visualise the scene as they listen and try to decide:
  ● the person's age
  ● the person's sex
  ● where the person is (describe the scene)
  ● why the person is lonely.
  Play the opening of the Verdi aria.

3 Ask your students what answers they would give to the questions in Step 2. Again encourage as many answers as possible and ask if they can explain their answers.

  Verdi was describing King Philip II of Spain (Queen Elizabeth I of England's great enemy) alone in his private chamber. His son, Don Carlos, has defied him. His wife does not love him. In middle age he has discovered that though he is king, no one loves him. In the aria that follows this introduction he sings of his intense loneliness.

4 Ask your class to think about occasions they have felt lonely and what caused the loneliness. Tell the class about an experience of yours. Then divide the class into groups of six to eight and ask them to talk in turns to the other members of their group about an experience of their own. While the groups are working, listen to as many students as possible. Provide any help they ask for, but don't interrupt the flow.

5 Tell the class you are going to play a second lonely piece, a piece by the Czech composer Dvořák, which he wrote while on a visit to America and when he was feeling very homesick for his native Czechoslovakia. Tell them that after this you will move on to solutions to loneliness. Play the music.

6 Move on to solutions to loneliness. Give an example from your own experience. Ask your students for further examples from their experience. These will fall basically into two categories: loneliness-avoidance tactics (diversion and distraction) and ways of learning to enjoy one's own company better (replacing loneliness by positive solitude). Make sure the students understand the difference.

OTHER SUGGESTED 'LONELY' MUSIC

1 Beethoven: Symphony No. 3 ('Eroica'), second movement. Beethoven had recently realised he was losing his hearing and heading for the loneliness of deafness.

2 R. Strauss: *Metamorphosen*. This agonised piece little by little metamorphoses a theme until it becomes the main theme of the second movement of Beethoven's 'Eroica' Symphony.

3 Frei Diogo da Conceição: 'Meio registo' for organ

4 Purcell: 'Dido's Lament' from *Dido and Aeneas*

5 Also, more recently in song:
  a) The Beatles: 'Eleanor Rigby'
  b) Ralph McTell: 'Streets of London'

8.5

LEVEL
Intermediate +

TIME
30 minutes in one lesson, plus 20 minutes per student in one or more further lessons

FOCUS
Discussion; Oral presentations to the class

EXTRAS
None

THE MUSIC THAT I AM

This activity provides an opportunity for you and your students to get to know one another and yourselves better through a piece of music. As it may reveal blind spots, use it only with classes where you feel a strong rapport with and within the group. For this reason it is best done with small classes (maximum of fifteen students).

Preparation

Choose a piece of music that you identify very closely with – one you feel in a sense could be a musical portrait of important things within you. If it is very long, select a representative section to play in class. Make a list of aspects of yourself that you hear in the music.

Procedure

1 Ask your students to think of and write down pieces of music they identify closely with. Ask them what aspects of themselves they feel the music reflects. Tell them to write brief notes about this – just a few words – beside each piece they have listed.

2 Tell the class you are going to play a piece of music you identify closely with. Ask them as they listen to write down what aspects of your character they feel they hear in the music.

3 Play the music.

4 Draw up two columns on the board. At the head of the first write *What the class hear*; at the head of the second *What I hear*. Ask the class for contributions to column 1 from what they wrote as they were listening. Write them on the board. Then write the list you prepared beforehand in column 2. Discuss with the class the differences between what they and you hear. Even if you don't fully agree with some of their comments, don't dismiss them. They may be offering you valuable insights.

5 Put it to the class that you would like each of them to present a piece of music in the way you have just done, a piece they wrote down in Step 1 above. Ask them how they feel about doing this. Be encouraging, but if you sense there are misgivings, discuss these openly and with understanding. If there is still strong resistance, be ready to abandon the idea. We have not yet found this necessary. If they agree to the idea, go on to Step 6.

6 Discuss with the students whether they want to concentrate their presentations over a few lessons and do nothing else in those lessons, or to spread them out over a longer period while doing other language work too in the same lessons. Work out with the class a schedule of who is going to give their presentation when.

7 Tell your students that when their turn comes you would like them to choose one of the pieces they identify closely with – one that they feel could be a musical portrait of important things within themselves. Tell them that if it is very long, you want them to select a section about ten minutes long to play to the class. Ask them also to make sure they bring a list of aspects of themselves they feel the music reflects. Tell them that just as you did for your own piece, you will ask everyone present to make a note of the aspects of the presenter's character they hear in the music and to compare this with the presenter's list.

8 In the lessons that follow, follow the same procedure as you did with your own piece (Steps 3 and 4), but with the students presenting their pieces, while you 'stage-manage' and respond to the needs that arise.

Bibliography

BT2 1988 *La Musique classique de l'Inde du Nord* (issue of a journal published by *PEMF*, BP 109 – F-06322 CANNES LA BOCCA CEDEX (France) in May 1988. (The clearest and most concise introduction to Indian music that we have come across)

Clapham, J 1972 *Smetana* (Master Musicians Series) Dent

Danielou, A 1985 *La musique de l'Inde du Nord* Buchet/Chastel (German and English translations available)

Daumal, R 1970 *Bharat: L'Origine du Théâtre, la Poésie et la Musique en Inde* Gallimard

Davis and Rinvolucri 1988 *Dictation – New Methods, New Possibilities* CUP

Demeure, R 1966 *A l'Ecoute des Oeuvres Musicales* Delagrave

Hirvela, A 1987 'Designing a Dog Exercising machine' in the English Teaching Forum, Vol xxv, 3, July 1987, pp 37–38

Institut für Auslandsbeziehungen, 1970 *Nationalhymnen* (Texte und Melodien) Philip Reclam Junior

Jones, L and Alexander, R 1989 *International Business English* CUP

Kennedy, M 1987 (3rd edition) *Portrait of Elgar* OUP

Krishnamurti, J 1973 *The Only Revolution* Gollancz

Laroy, C 1991 Music in Humanistic Language Teaching. Acts of *I Congrés Internacional sobre l'Ensenyament de Llengües Estrangeres*, Universitat Autònoma de Barcelona, Institut de Ciènces de l'Educació

Lehmann, D 1988 *Music in Suggestopedia* (translated and adapted with comments by Sigrid Gassner-Roberts) University of Adelaide, Australia

Lozanov, G 1979 *Suggestology and Outlines of Suggestopedy* Gordon and Breach Science Publishers Ltd

McArthur, R 1981 *Longman Lexicon* Longman

Moskowitz, G 1978 *Caring and Sharing in the Foreign Language Class* Newbury House

Opie, I and P 1951 *The Oxford Dictionary of Nursery Rhymes* OUP

Opie, I and P 1955 *The Oxford Nursery Rhyme Book* OUP

Prokofiev, D 1942 *Peter and the Wolf* Boosey and Hawkes

Rodale, J I 1947 *The Word Finder* Rodale Press

Satie, E (illustrated Martin, C.) 1982 *Sports et divertissements* Dover Publications (facsimile of edition by Publications Lucien Vogel)

Storr, A 1976 *The Dynamics of Creation* Penguin Books Ltd

Further reading

Campbell, D 1983 *Introduction to the Musical Brain* MMB Music Inc

Carron, W, Geerolf, L, Isselee, J-P 1974 (2nd edition) *Muziek Beluisteren: programmamuziek* De Sikkel (Antwerpen)

Cranmer, D 1990 Variations on a Musical Theme *Practical English Teaching* 11 (1) September

Daniélou, A 1959 *Traité de musicologie comparée* Hermann

Daniélou, A 1978 *Sémantique musicale – Essai de psychophysiologie auditive* Hermann

Ethnomusicology (Journal of the Society for Ethnomusicology) Morrison Hall 005, Indiana University

Guilhot, J and M-A, Jost, J, Lecourt, E 1977 *La Musicothérapie et les méthodes nouvelles d'association des techniques* ESF

Guiraud-Caladou, J-M 1983 *Musicothérapie, parole des maux* Van de Velde

Hamel, P M 1980 *Durch Musik zum Selbst*, wie man Musik neu erleben und erfahren kann – Bärenreiter (Kassel) & DTV

Jackendoff, R 1987 *Consciousness and the Computational Mind* MIT Press

Kwabena Nketia, J H 1975 *The Music of Africa* Gollancz

Lallemand, J 1928 *L'Emotion musicale normale* – Thèse pour le doctorat en médecine défendue le 11/3/1887 Vigné

Liedtke, R 1984 *Die Vertreibung der Stille* Schönberger (1988 DTV)

Mulder, E 1985 *Muziek in Spiegelbeeld*, Essays over muziekfilosofie en dieptepsychologie Ambo

Renner, H and Schweizer, K 1985 *Reclams Konzertführer* Philip Reclam jun.

Rudhyar, D 1982 *The Magic of Tone and the Art of Music* Shambala Publications (exists in German: DTV)

Sloboda, J 1985 *The Musical Mind: The Cognitive Psychology of Music* OUP

Werner-Jensen, A 1990 *Reclams Kammermusikführer* Philip Reclam jun.

Cassette contents

CHAPTER 1

1.3 Vaughan Williams: Fantasia on 'Greensleeves' – 'Lovely Joan' theme
Rodrigo: *Fantasia para un gentilhombre* (second movement)

1.6 Rossini: Overture to *The Thieving Magpie* (crescendo)

1.8 Susato Collection 1551: 'La Morisque'

CHAPTER 3

3.2 Saint-Saëns: *Le Rouet d'Omphale* (finale)
Vaughan Williams: *Sinfonia Antartica* (fifth movement)
Grieg: *Peer Gynt* – 'Peer Gynt Hunted by the Trolls'

3.5 Ravel: *Le Tombeau de Couperin* (Menuet)

3.6 R. Strauss: *Also sprach Zarathustra* (opening)
Berlioz: *Symphonie Fantastique* (last section of fourth movement)
Beethoven: Symphony No. 5 (opening)

3.7 Mozart: Piano Concerto No. 21 in C Major (second movement)
Nielsen: Symphony No. 6 (opening of first movement)

3.8 Saint-Saëns: *Carnival of the Animals* – 'The Swan'
Sibelius: *The Swan of Tuonela* (opening)

CHAPTER 4

4.1 Verdi: *Un ballo in maschera* (Act I Sc II opening)
Wagner: *Das Rheingold* – 'Descent to Niebelheim'
Wagner: *Tristan und Isolde* (opening of Prelude)
Rimsky-Korsakov: Quintet in B flat (opening of third movement)

4.5 Holst: *The Planets* – 'Mars' (finale)

CHAPTER 5

5.1 Nielsen: Symphony No. 2 – 'The Four Temperaments' (second movement)

5.3 J. S. Bach: Brandenburg Concerto No. 6 (first movement)
Pachelbel: Canon in D
Bruch: Violin Concerto No. 1 in G minor (opening of second movement)

5.7 Elgar: *Enigma Variations;* Variation 7 – 'Troyte', Variation 8 – 'W.N.', Variation 9 – 'Nimrod'

CHAPTER 6

6.5 Khatchaturian: Piano Concerto (second movement)

CHAPTER 7

7.1 Vivaldi: Piccolo Concerto in C major (first movement)
Handel: Organ Concerto No. 4 in F (opening of first movement)
Mahler: Symphony No. 1 in D minor (opening of fourth movement)

7.4 Satie: *Sports et divertissements* – 'La pêche'

7.5 Satie: *Sports et divertissements* – 'Le pique-nique'

CHAPTER 8

8.2 Excerpt from the *alap* of an Indian raga
   Albinoni: Adagio for organ and Strings
   Verdi: *Rigoletto* – 'La donna è mobile' (orchestral introduction and
      beginning of the aria)
8.4 Verdi: *Don Carlos* – aria 'Ella giammai m'amo' (solo cello opening)